ON THE
BORDERS
OF
CRIME

ON THE BORDERS OF CRIME

Conflict Management
and
Criminology

LESLIE W. KENNEDY

UNIVERSITY OF ALBERTA

Longman
New York & London

On the Borders of Crime: Conflict Management and Criminology

Longman, 95 Church Street, White Plains, N.Y. 10601
A division of Addison-Wesley Publishing Co., Inc.

Associated companies:
Longman Group Ltd., London
Longman Cheshire Pty., Melbourne
Longman Paul Pty., Auckland
Copp Clark Pitman, Toronto

Senior editor: David J. Estrin
Production editor: Ann P. Kearns
Cover design: Jill Francis Wood
Production supervisor: Kathleen M. Ryan

Library of Congress Cataloging-in-Publication Data

Kennedy, Leslie W.
    On the borders of crime: conflict management and criminology / by
Leslie W. Kennedy.
        p.   cm.
    Bibliography: p.
    Includes index.
    ISBN 0-8013-0151-3
    1. Crime and criminals.   2. Social conflict.   3. Interpersonal conflict.
4. Conflict management.   1. Title.
HV6025.K29   1990
364—dc19

                                                                  88-36450
                                                                       CIP

ABCDEFGHIJ-DO-99 98   97   96   95   94   93   92   91   90

To Ilona, Alexis, Andrea, and grandparents

Contents

Introduction

My first introduction to the role that informal control can play in managing social behavior came during a justice tour of China in 1981. Throughout the tour, we were reminded that crime and delinquency do not occur only when formal agencies, such as the police, become involved. Rather, as it was explained to us by judges, lawyers, factory supervisors, and leaders of neighborhood mediation programs, much misbehavior occurs outside of the influence of these agencies and must be confronted and controlled through informal means available to the community. The informal processes of mediation and conflict management practiced by the community outside of the courts are important ways of reducing these problems.

The Chinese experience has come to the attention of North Americans, who are faced with overcrowded and sometimes unresponsive courts. There is a general appreciation that a large part of the problem of social disorder comes from a breakdown of informal social support and the overreliance on formal adjudication. Mediation programs have sprung up across North America as a way of reinstituting conflict management outside of the courts. These programs have had some success, as we will see in our review, but they are confronted with problems of low community cohesion, which makes them less desirable.

At the same time as these mediation programs have been offered as a way to manage community conflict, we find that the police have begun to turn to new ways of addressing the roots of social disorder that lead to crime. Community-based policing, which involves the police in community problems, uses local resources to reduce crime. In a similar way, courts are looking for alternative ways to deter offenders without incarceration while recognizing the call by the public to get tough on crime.

All these trends have left us to question whether or not our contemporary approaches to defining crime depict this behavior in realistic terms. The increased demand for theories that focus on psychological determinants of criminality force us to ignore its social origins. The emphasis on crime as a social fact precludes a consideration of crime as a product of conflict, with the borders around the criminal act predetermined rather than negotiated. This book will examine conflict-based crime and the factors that determine how criminality comes to be defined from this perspective in contrast to that offered by "conservative" approaches, which emphasize narrow (and, to my mind, incomplete) explanations. We will review the Chinese experience but draw, as well, on examples from the United States, Canada, and Great Britain to help illustrate how these various ideas have influenced our response to crime.

This book is not intended as a review of all existing criminological theories, although the important ones (including social learning, subcultural, and labeling theories) are discussed in the context of the arguments made about conflict-based criminology. There are some excellent reviews of these theories presented elsewhere, including Nettler's *Explaining Crime* and Vold and Bernard's *Theoretical Criminology*. I hope that this book will inspire debate about how the link between conflict and crime comes to define and redefine our views of criminality and the ways in which we respond to it. This book is directed at undergraduates who are receiving their first exposure to crime and criminal justice responses to it. I hope that the ideas raised here will encourage further study of these issues. An extensive bibliography is presented at the end of the book for those interested in pursuing certain concepts in greater detail.

I have a number of people to thank for their contributions to this work. My wife, Ilona, spent many hours reading and analyzing the text in its early, and less comprehensible, stage. I owe her a lot for her careful comments and unflagging support. Others have spent hours helping me to improve the ideas and their delivery. Bob Silverman has been a long-time colleague, collaborator, and friend. He brought criminological sense to the text. David Forde, a new friend and colleague, read the manuscript twice and helped improve it both times. Rick Linden, Karyn Mytrash, and Marianne Nielsen provided important insights on different ideas that they felt needed to be better explained, and Craig McEwan's reaction to the mediation section was invaluable. Jack Clark, a fellow China traveler, was an important inspiration in bringing this book to print. Finally, the patience and enthusiasm of my editor, David Estrin, and his staff at Longman have helped me concentrate on getting the manuscript to its final stage, to you, the reader.

CHAPTER 1

Social Conflict on the Borders of Crime

INTRODUCTION

In Western society, crime is defined strictly as behavior that breaks the law and is liable to public prosecution and punishment. This definition allows us to treat crime as a phenomenon separate from other social factors. We start with the criminal event, explaining it by creating fixed definitional boundaries around it. Using this definition, we can prescribe fixed responses to crime through the administration of justice. Theories of crime can then be developed after classifications of the social forms and factors associated with criminal behavior are created (Cain & Kulscar, 1981–82: 386). This approach is preclusive, creating artificial borders around crime, and discourages criminologists from addressing the conflict beyond these boundaries that may have contributed to the development of the crime in the first place. There is, then, no need to address the fact that these boundaries change through negotiation of what constitutes criminal behavior both in the ways individuals respond to it and in the ways the criminal justice system tries to control it.

Sellin (1938) cautions that the unqualified acceptance of **legal** definitions of the basic units or elements of criminological inquiry violates a fundamental criterion of science. The scientist must be free to define his or her own terms. Confinement to the study of crime and criminals as laid down in law renders criminological research theoretically invalid from the point of view of science (Sellin, 1938: 24). What is needed, instead, is an approach to crime in which the definitions of criminal behavior may change

1

and evolve depending on the nature of the interactions among individuals and those between them and the agencies that administer control over social behavior.

How we define the problem of crime can point to its root causes or can lead us to deal only with its symptoms. We must know not only **what** these definitions entail but also **how** definitions of crime are developed. Further, the negotiation of justice may be a reflection not only of what the agents of social control **can do** but also what they are **prepared to do** in attacking crime.

The definitions of crime through law may be seen as unchangeable, determined by the rules of evidence in establishing guilt or innocence. Alternatively, law can be seen as defining the boundaries of behavior that is unacceptable depending on circumstance, public tolerance, and judicial discretion. Agents of social control use the law not only to deter crime and punish criminals but also to reduce social conflict. Some behavior not dealt with through the formal application of law may be disorderly, threatening, or dangerous. Any study of crime needs to account for behavior that has these characteristics but is not yet unlawful. Further, some of this disorderly behavior has not been handled by the police or courts, either because it has not come to their attention or because they have chosen to ignore it. Alternate responses, such as community-based mediation, have developed in society to deal with these problems, which often stretch beyond the resources of the police and courts but which still pose a threat to social order. Alternative, or informal, responses have to be accounted for, even though they do not elicit any specific legal sanction. They create the outside limits of criminality by redefining the response of criminal justice to misbehavior.

It will be argued in this book that crime has its roots in conflict, and a number of questions will be addressed: Are the factors that contribute to the emergence of conflict the same factors that contribute to the development of crime? When does crime detach itself from the social disorder that comes with conflict, if at all? Does this result in a separate social phenomenon that can be treated and eradicated outside of the influence of social conflict?

This rest of this chapter will address the general issues relating to boundary formation for criminal behavior, setting the stage for the detailed treatment of conflict and our response to it. We will begin by dealing with the **normalcy** and **inevitability** of conflict and crime, in terms of both public acceptance of social disorder and social control. Our tolerance for the occurrence of criminality will affect where the lines are drawn in the definitions of this behavior. Lack of tolerance can be manifested in our willingness to invoke formal intervention in confronting misbehavior. On the other hand, the nonreporting of crime can reflect a willingness to define behavior as operating within the bounds of informal response, not requiring criminalization for resolution.

We will also examine the bases under which law operates in conflicts, providing outlines of how acceptable and unacceptable behavior can evolve. Law is an instrument wielded by agents of social control. How these agents use the law, including their interpretation of discretionary action, must be considered in any definition of criminality. The application of law can also influence the effects of coercion, deterrence, and punishment in constraining misbehavior. Let us begin our discussion by focusing on the factors that influence how society defines the boundaries between crime and conflict.

SETTING THE BORDERS OF CRIME

Crime and Conflict as Normal in Society

It is true that not all conflict results in serious crime.[1] A great deal of conflict is expressed through less harmful forms of misbehavior. By focusing on conflict as a factor in promoting violence, we do not deny the pathology that can lead to individual murders or other forms of criminal violence. We do create, however, an opportunity to study the underlying **social factors** that contribute to this violence.

Nettler (1984a) argues that the idea of crime starts with some conception of proper behavior. This conception is based on **morality**, whereby a society establishes general rules of acceptable or **normative** behavior. As Nettler states, morals change, and with the changes are variations in the content of crime. "The broad boundaries of offenses against property, person, and 'society' remain fairly steady, but the criminal content within these boundaries varies" (Nettler, 1984a:2). Defining normative behavior is confounded by our reactions to the behavior that occurs with changes in morality. With what frequency must a type of act occur before it is considered a norm (Gibbs, 1981:14)? Further, what percentage of agreement do we need in the population to guarantee that the public would see certain behavior as acceptable (Gibbs, 1981:11)? Similarly, what level of punishment is necessary to guarantee that we have reached an optimal level of

---

[1] Serious crime has been defined by Wilson and Herrnstein (1985) as homicide, rape, serious assault, and robbery. We will add to this list serious property offenses, including grand theft, burglary, and arson.

social order (Currie, 1985)? What level of enforcement of laws ensures that we have safe streets and homes?

The concern (see Currie, 1985) about the "unacceptably" high levels of crime in the United States is put into the context of what occurs in other countries. Of note here are the substantially lower levels of serious crime in Canada, most particularly homicide, which is a quarter the rate of that in the United States. Canada is a country which is in many ways similar to the United States. When Canadians compare themselves to Americans, they see their level of crime as generally more acceptable. However, when considered in their own right within the country, these lower rates in Canada are still considered to be too high.

When setting levels of acceptable social disorder there may be a cultural phenomenon operating whereby socially **legitimate use** of violence can affect the degree to which **illegitimate and criminal** violence occurs (Straus, 1985). In the United States, factors such as preference for violent television programs; participation in socially approved violent activities, including college football; and the use of corporal punishment in schools exhibit regional differences, with higher levels in the West and South. These high levels of legitimate violence are correlated with high levels of homicide. The acceptable levels of crime, then, may actually vary regionally, depending on the values people place on the legitimate use of physical force. Public support for violence may be complemented by public support for enforcement. As Straus (1985) reports, there are regional variations in the support for capital punishment, as well. In addition, tolerance of legitimate violence may be higher nationwide in the United States than in other countries.

Acceptable social behavior, then, is circumscribed by an overlay of morality. Behavior that falls outside of these normative boundaries does not disappear but rather takes on a different character as crime. Crime of some sort is evident in all societies. This fact has led some scholars to argue that crime itself is an inevitable part of the development of social control (Durkheim, 1964).

Crime and Conflict as Inevitable

Two differing approaches to the inevitability of crime are offered by Durkheim and by Quinney (Hilbert & Wright, 1982). Durkheim (1964) argues that behavior defined as crime in society can be eliminated only by the most successful kind of socialization. The sentiments underlying any particular law would have to be implanted uniformly in all individuals and with an intensity sufficient to deter the expression of all desires to the contrary, a goal that Durkheim considers impossible to attain. If crime is conceived of as a serious violation of the collective conscience, it cannot be eliminated by strengthening the grip that conscience has on the group. The definition of what is criminal will simply change to accommodate more rigid definitions of moral failings.

For Quinney (1974), crime need not be inevitable. Law, he argues, is an instrument of coercion whereby groups are subordinated through the use of political power (Hilbert & Wright, 1982:75). The conflict of divergent interests in capitalist states leads to crime being defined as action operating against the interests of the dominant class. This crime, Quinney argues, occurs between groups. If group distinctions and interests were to disappear, as he would argue they would in a socialist state, crime would disappear. There would be general agreement on principles and therefore no need for law.

A provocative element of the Quinney argument revolves around the belief that community custom would prevail in societies free of conflict and crime. He uses the example of the community tribunal, which enforces custom as a way of resolving community disputes and educating the public (Quinney, 1974:191). This process releases one from relying on law to define what behavior is criminal.

The contrast between Durkheim and Quinney can be summarized as follows. Durkheim argues that crime results from the fact that society is an imperfect moral order. The effort to strengthen the grip of the collective conscience is self-defeating as this attempt simply redefines behavior and creates more crime. Quinney, on the other hand, views society as segmented, with law as an outgrowth of conflicts of interest. With the breakdown of segmentation, conflict will disappear and crime will be eliminated. "Crime is not a function of consensus (Durkheim) but a lack thereof (Quinney)..." (Hilbert & Wright, 1982:83).

The weakness in these arguments on the inevitability of crime revolves around the definition of what is criminal. As Hilbert and Wright state, changing from law to custom does not suggest that deviant behavior will be eliminated but only that it will no longer be illegal. This view of crime does not recognize the fundamental elements of conflict that remain in society and thus form the bases for interpersonal disputes, whether defined as criminal or not. The struggle for power or the attempt to provide socialization for conformity to societal norms clearly helps explain different aspects of this dispute-based process. The commonality of disputes in both theories (only to be dealt with through informal versus formal means, according to the ideological brand of society) underlies the point that it may be social conflict that is inevitable, with crime as a less predictable outgrowth of the legal interpretations of the consequences of personal disputes.

How "Hidden Crime" Further Defines
the Borders of Crime and Conflict

Confounding our view of what is criminal is the observation that only a small proportion of crime actually comes to the attention of the police. The nonreporting of crime, referred to as the *dark figure,* created a great sensation when the high levels were confirmed in victimization studies (Skogan, 1984). In the U.S. National Crime Survey conducted in 1979, victims were asked why they failed to report crimes. The single most frequent reason for not reporting was that they felt that the offense was not important enough to warrant police attention. The second most important reason given was the feeling that nothing could be done to right the wrong they had suffered. The sense of fear, personal powerlessness, and threats of further victimization from authority are all factors that contribute to the lack of action toward crime (Kidd & Chayet, 1984).

There is also an indication that failure to report may occur because of the involvement of the victim with the offender, for example, in cases of sexual assault. The victim may be too embarrassed to bring the offense to the attention of the courts because of fear of publicity. There are also the cases in which the victim does not sympathize with the possible penal sanctions that are to be imposed as a result of reporting (McClintock, 1970). In these cases, the victims may simply choose to ignore the offense or resolve it themselves. In addition, individuals may not consider themselves victims at all. The process of defining an offender and victim may not be consistent with the actual circumstances of the quarrel or conflict with other persons. The police may stay out or be kept out because of the decision made by the individuals involved that the retribution enacted on the spot was fair and equitable (Kennedy, 1988).

What is not well understood are the factors that prevent certain behaviors from being dealt with as criminal (even though legally they may have these attributes). The fact that they are not reported makes them no less criminal. Yet there are other dimensions to this problem that need to be addressed. Are those behaviors that are reported substantially different from those that are not? Is their nonreporting a function of inadequate policing, poor courts, or frightened victims? Or is it possible that this non-reporting is a clue to the origins of many crimes? That is, do these crimes have their roots in ongoing social behavior, and as a result, are they resolved through informal means available to victims? Further, what does this nonreporting say about the characteristics of offenders and the ways in which they act in response to the informal controls that exist in society? How important are the characteristics of victims and the nature of the interrelationship between them and offenders? We will address these questions in detail in Chapter 3.

SEARCHING FOR LAW IN CONFLICT

Legal Definitions of Crime and Conflict

Crime and our response to crime are really two sides of the same coin (Vold & Bernard, 1986). Criminal definitions are a product of social conflict and change but are often administered with discretion by agencies of social control. We need to consider how conflict can shift the **boundaries** of what the justice system treats as crime, that is, behavior requiring judicial reaction. In our effort to establish these borders of crime, we will try to identify the major factors that contribute to the development of rule making and the process of settlement that adherence to the law requires.

To understand the consequences that well-established law has on social behavior, we must look beyond the abstract statements of rules to the actions of people who use these rules in resolving conflict. How do the social conditions operating on them affect the ways in which they deal with disputes? Also, does the application of the stated rule always have the intended effect on disputants' behavior? In studies of children, Maynard suggests that the conflict they experience actually helps them create social organization. The conflict process makes children aware of social order, control mechanisms, and political process. In addition, this conflict functions latently to reproduce authority, friendship, and other interactional patterns that transcend single episodes of dispute (Maynard, 1985:220). Conflict works, then, to test the .boundaries of acceptability in interpersonal relations.

The informal management of conflict, through processes such as negotiation or mediation, becomes an important counterpoint to the formal structure of control provided by the state (Nader, 1984:88). Western jurisprudence treats as criminal only those things done on purpose, that is, with *mens rea*.[2] Other cultures include for punishment things that we would consider accidents. This difference is especially well illustrated in the conflict that emerges between Native American and white society in North America. Where Native American culture allows for informal social control and emphasis on group conformity through negotiation, the formal rule making of white society does not. Certain behavior that would elicit reimbursement or replacement in Native American society may call for punishment in white society. The lack of understanding of formal rules can

---

[2] This rule does not excuse all accidents in which, with constructive intent, individuals may do damage to others through negligence or neglect. The accidents caused by drunk drivers, for example, although not intentional, are caused by individuals who did not take proper care to control their behavior. They are, therefore, deemed criminal.

help explain the problems faced by Native American offenders (Nielsen, 1982). The reliance on process versus outcome in Native justice makes this group more vulnerable to conflict with the rules of white society.

It is possible, further, that low tolerance for conflict may lead to **overregulation** of behavior. This may result, in turn, in the redefinition of conflicts to be dealt with in more formal ways (i.e., through the courts) when previously these disputes were resolved informally. This demand for formal justice invokes the concept of an "overreach of the law" in cases in which more acceptable solutions may come from informal resources available to the antagonists (Morris & Hawkins, 1969). High crime rates may occur because we overcriminalize certain behavior. For example, there is no clear agreement on whether or not a crime can be, in fact, victimless. It has been argued that we need not criminalize in cases in which there are no victims, for example, prostitution and drug addiction (Schur, 1965). This argument illustrates the disagreement that exists concerning not only the levels but also the types of behavior that need to be treated in criminal terms.

Criminalization creates its own reactions, sometimes promoting instead of controlling criminality. Witness the industry that has sprung up around some crimes, such as drug abuse and gambling. These types of deviance often create more crime than the original misbehavior. The overreach of the law is debated later in this book in the context of managing community conflict through formal and informal resolution.

The state may resolve to deal harshly with certain crimes but not have the means to accomplish it. Establishing guilt may not ensure punishment. Being liable to prosecution and punishment is clearly not the same as actually being prosecuted and punished (Hagan, 1985:32). Problems arise in our enforcement of the laws, in our reporting of illegal behavior, and in our prosecution and punishment of known offenders. In addition there are problems of punishing the misbehavior that occurs outside the formal agencies' rule. Discretion is often used in reporting or resolving these "crimes." Crime comes to be defined, then, as part of the ongoing negotiation that occurs in society between groups that are victims of crime and those that actually perpetrate it; between offenders and the institutions that control or deter criminal behavior; and between the public and the lawmakers who set out the guidelines for enforcement.

Models to Manage Conflict and Crime: Chinese Examples

The importance of rules in dispute settlement has been illustrated in cross-cultural analysis of jurisprudence (Kidder, 1983). Early anthropological research sought to define how social order is maintained in primitive societies. As Kidder points out, anthropologists felt that the ways in which disputes in society are managed would help illustrate how individuals confront the world. "Anthropologists felt that trouble cases could expose elements of a culture's view of the world which are normally hidden when relationships proceed according to routine" (Kidder, 1983:160), providing a view of how societies adjust their rules to fit changing circumstances.

Despite differences in detail and sociocultural context, we can learn from the experience of other countries that have dealt directly with the link between formal and informal forms of social control. Comparisons across culture are precarious, however. Even though some argue that the management of disputes is essentially the same across all cultures (Gulliver, 1979:261), others claim that this is not the case and we should not attempt to draw solutions for the negotiation of disputes freely from other societies (Cain & Kulscar, 1981–82). Despite the problems encountered in cross-national comparisons, it is useful to examine the experiences of other societies. The country that has caught the attention of legal scholars and social scientists alike is China, where for centuries there have been complementary forms of formal and informal justice. We can use this example to illustrate how law and informal justice can operate together in maintaining social order.

Leng (1977) points out that two models of law have coexisted and competed with one another in the People's Republic of China: the jural (formal) model and the societal (informal) model. This dichotomy in law can be compared to *Fa* (positive law) and *Li* (moral code), which were used in traditional China to regulate human behavior and social order. Confucius had a low opinion of law that was conceived of as sets of rules designed to prohibit people from doing wrong:

> If the people are governed by laws and their conduct is regulated by a system of punishments they will only try to avoid punishment, and will lose the sense of shame. On the other hand, if the people are governed by morality, and their conduct is regulated by rules of Li, they will have the sense of shame amd will also become good. (Chai & Chai, 1962:102)

Confucius ranked *Li* above *Fa* for the regulation of public and private behavior.

In contemporary China, as in traditional China, formal rules have played a secondary role. The jural model represents formal, elaborate, and codified rules enforced by a centralized and institutionalized bureaucracy. In contrast, the societal model operates with socially approved norms and values, implemented by political socialization and enforced by social pressures (Leng, 1977:357).

Part of the rationale behind the support of the societal model derives from a distinctly Maoist approach to law. In Mao's writings and government there was deep suspicion of the bureaucratic rule. Mao emphasized informality and flexibility in handling political and legal issues. His feeling about informality did not prevent his government from setting up a judicial process. But the emphasis remained on the invocation of responsibility to the masses when applying sanctions and settling disputes.

After the Chinese Revolution, the dual models of law operated in a complementary yet competitive manner. With economic development in the 1950s, there was a general swing toward institutionalization and bureaucratic normalization. This trend stopped with the antirightist campaign in 1957. The judiciary and procuracy (prosecution) declined, to the point that in 1966, the Cultural Revolution completely disabled the formal legal system and Mao disbanded the procuracy, leaving law enforcement in the hands of the military.

The 1975 constitution contributed further to the decline of the jural model and its emphasis on due process (e.g., equality before the law, public trials, right to defense, and protection against arbitrary arrest). More recently, however, the Chinese have created the first comprehensive code of substantive or procedural criminal law. With the new constitution of 1978, the legal omissions of the 1975 constitution were reinstated. Among those revived are the rights of the accused to defense and to an open, public trial and the participation of the people's assessor in the administration of justice (Cohen, 1982:206). The constitution also reinstates the procuracy and reestablishes the requirement for the police to have the approval of the judiciary or the procuracy before making an arrest.

Cohen (1982) indicates that the old ways are not dying out quickly and the rule of law as outlined in the new code is not yet applied universally. A great deal of reliance is still made of the informal (societal) model. Cohen, Leng, and Chieu (1977:329) make the point that the resources available to the criminal process are limited, in personnel as well as in finances.

> In view of the country's vast population and area, it has long been recognized that an immense and cumbersome state apparatus would be required to process all criminal cases and to impose sanctions against all offenders. Thus today, as in imperial China, the state's burden is shared by consigning the handling of many anti-social acts to persons other than officials. (Cohen, Leng, & Chieu, 1977:329)

These observations indicate a functional as well as an ideological basis for the use of local groups to provide societal control. Many minor acts that might otherwise be deemed criminal are often considered and disposed of on the spot by unofficial persons, such as members of an agricultural production team or a factory workshop, neighborhood residents, or even an ad hoc cluster of bystanders. Cohen, and colleagues state that this custom has the traditional virtue of conserving state resources and allowing local groups to deal with many of their own problems (Cohen, Leng, & Chieu, 1977:329). The process is further facilitated by the strong family traditions still prevalent in China, whereby the family is seen as the major focus of social control, and the government structure is based on political units that operate with some autonomy in managing local affairs.

Also, there is a general lack of transiency among the population. Migration is difficult throughout the country and occurs only with the sponsorship of a factory or government agency. The family and the local unit take responsibility for the actions of their members and are held responsible for their misdeeds.

"Study" groups, in which most Chinese participate, discuss and settle problems involving minor infractions by their members. Certain citizens have been selected to serve on a part-time volunteer basis to mediate disputes. They are also involved in reducing social disorder, often in cooperation with the police. These citizens are looked to for leadership in dealing with minor public disorder because of their responsibilities for production, education, neighborhood administration, or Communist Party or Youth League work. They will consult with the police officer on the urban beat and the officer assigned to maintain contact between a rural commune and the county Public Security Bureau (police) if there is doubt about the proper course of action. At the same time the police can divert to the appropriate group minor cases that have come to their attention (Cohen, Leng, & Chieu, 1977:329–330).

The Chinese experience with complementary systems of formal and informal social control has come to the attention of North American legal scholars as offering a way in which social disorder can be controlled through an expansion of social intervention in the face of restricted resources for judicial response. We will examine this strategy in greater detail in Chapter 5, where we review mediation programs.

SUMMARY

Crime is set in a sea of conflict. Defining the borders of crime depends on our view of the "normalcy" of crime, that is, the extent to which we accept the breach of law. Boundary maintenance may depend on the general tolerance for conflict and the degree to which we see certain crime as inevitable, requiring legal versus extralegal (community-based) responses. Much of this public acceptance of the normalcy and inevitability of crime is reflected in the extent of nonreporting of lawbreaking. The failure to report is due in part to fear and powerlessness but also results from a sense that certain misbehavior or disagreements have been resolved. These conflicts need not, therefore, come to the attention of formal agencies.

Conflict may provide an integrative function, defining clearly the rules or laws that need to be applied in controlling behavior. When these rules are broken, however, the conflict takes on a different form, becoming criminal. Conflict brings out the need for the application of rules that might have remained dormant and forgotten had no conflict occurred. "...Like boundary stones between proprietors who have never quarreled over boundary lines...conflict thus intensifies participation in social life" (Coser, 1956:127).

The breaking of rules by one group may be promoted through identification with subcultural values that conflict with those of the majority. This can be seen as conflict as defined by the "new" criminologists (see Taylor, Walton, & Young, 1973), that political power criminalizes the economically underprivileged. Or this conflict may simply be seen as a low-intensity disagreement that exists between floating coalitions of business people, children, or neighbors. It may take on political overtones when a politically weak group does not define it as crime, for example, marijuana use (Vold & Bernard, 1986:292). It can also have its roots in basic disagreements over rights and obligations that may come from differences in ethnic or racial background (Merry, 1979).

The administration of law incoporates the view that law can be negotiated and has at its roots the rules of society, which promote negotiation and mediation of conflict that can become crime. The model of formal and informal control combining to define acceptable behavior and acceptable responses to misbehavior, as illustrated in the Chinese experience, provides an important framework for studying the ways in which boundaries are formed to create crime. In this book, we advocate the view that crime is not an isolated social fact but rather a social construct that has moral, legal, economic, political, and social roots. Criminological theories must account for those factors that link crime to conflict. These ideas must now be tested in the context of criminological theories that have taken as given the phenomenon of crime as an isolated social construct. The importance of a social conflict perspective in broadening the scope of these theories now needs to be examined.

CHAPTER 2
Linking Conflict and Crime: Theoretical Questions

INTRODUCTION

It is common for criminology texts to introduce theories of crime on their own merits, criticizing each perspective as it is presented. The student is normally exposed, then, first to biological theories, to psychological theories, and then to the myriad of criminological theories deriving from sociological explanations of crime. Given the specific focus of this book, it seems appropriate that these different theories be introduced in the context of how they address conflict in relationship to crime. This task will be facilitated by reviewing the controversy that has developed around the recent publication of *Crime and Human Nature* by James Q. Wilson and Richard Herrnstein. This work, which revives explanations from the early 1900s of criminality based on constitutional defects of offenders, has been likened to a "flank attack" on theories of crime that emphasize the importance of social conditions, such as ethnicity, family structure, or poverty, in creating social disorder (Gibbs, 1985:381). The debate that the Wilson and Herrnstein book has generated helps to highlight the points for and against an approach to crime that incorporates an understanding of conflict.

In this chapter, we will examine how explanations based on social conflict differ in their predictions of crime incidence compared to more narrow perspectives that focus only on specific characteristics of offenders. To represent the latter, we will highlight the arguments made in support of the conservative (or "constitutional") model of criminal behavior, comparing it to the conflict-based approach in the conceptualization of factors that contribute to crime, at the individual, group, and institutional level. Toward this end, we will review the debates over the relative importance of heredity versus socialization, personality versus social situation, and criminal predispositions versus group processes.

HEREDITY VERSUS SOCIALIZATION

Constitution versus Social Circumstance in Predicting Criminality

In reviewing theories of criminality, Wilson and Herrnstein argue that crime is best explained through the interaction between biological traits of offenders and the conditioning effects of the social environment in which they live. Their most contentious argument is that there is a strong case to be made for differences in body type predicting the ways in which individuals weigh the rewards and costs of criminal behavior. Wilson and Herrnstein conclude that the larger the ratio of the rewards (material and nonmaterial) of noncrime to the rewards (material and nonmaterial) of crime, the weaker the tendency to commit crime. They say that the average offender tends to be constitutionally distinctive, though not extremely or subnormally so: "The biological factors whose traces we see in faces, physiques, and correlation with behavior of parents and siblings are predispositions towards crime that are expressed as psychological traits and activated by circumstance" (Wilson & Herrnstein, 1985:103). This approach to criminality is similar to explanations offered by the social control theorists, who argue that criminal behavior results from defective social training in lawful standards of conduct (Hirschi, 1969). However, where it differs is in the emphasis that Wilson and Herrnstein give to the role of genetics, IQ, and personality.

In contrast to this perspective, Sutherland argued that every explanation of crime production rests on a notion of conflict. Crime arises when there are disagreements between interests when laws are enacted and punishments exacted to maintain and protect these interests (Sutherland, 1929). For example, economists who look at theft as rational are conflict theorists in the sense that they observe some people wanting and taking what others have. Similarly, subcultural theorists who look at crime as produced by people of different tastes living together under one law are also using an explanation emphasizing conflict (Nettler, 1984a:186). In a broader sense, social psychologists who stress the causal importance of opportunities, interpretations of situations, or training regimes all rest their explanations of crime on some sort of conflict. "For all these many theorists, conflict resides in differences—whether the differences be in opportunities, in ideas, or in nurturing" (Nettler, 1984a:186).

Broadening our approach to include conflict[1] challenges certain basic assumptions made in "conservative" criminology. This debate crosses a variety of criminological perspectives based on social factors, including **subcultural**, **labeling**, **social control**, and **conflict theories**, addressing the ways in which each school of thought accounts for social conflict in its explanation of crime. The general disagreement between conservative and conflict-based criminology is well illustrated in the differences in interpretation of the origins of family violence.

The Case of Family Violence: Learned or Inherited?

The proponents of a conservative model of crime, such as that proposed by Wilson and Herrnstein (1985) and Wilson (1983), advocate that "it makes no sense to talk about the social or 'root' causes of crime at all, either because such causes do not exist or because no one knows what they are or how to find them" (Currie, 1985:23). Wilson and Herrnstein reject sociological explanations of crime, arguing that they direct attention away from individual differences and toward "abstract" categories. Social forces, they say, cannot deter 100 percent of the population from committing crime. Thus the distributions of crime within and across societies must reflect underlying distributions of constitutional factors. Research on twins and adoptees that searches for genetic predispositions to crime (see, for example, Mednick et al., 1984) have provided quite compelling evidence on crime trends related to genetic makeup, especially in tracking the differential effects of birth parents versus adoptive parents in intergenerational tendencies toward crime. However, what is left unanswered in this research is whether behaviorally based propensities are actually directed toward precursors to crime, such as alcoholism, rather than criminal intent itself.

Wilson and Herrnstein (1985), reviewing the literature on domestic violence, try to support the view that violence is inherited, thus dismissing the relationship between social conditions and criminality. They point out that there is strong evidence that abusive homes produce more aggressive children. There are, then, good reasons for supposing that early aggres-

---

[1] The non-Marxist approach to conflict-based criminology is well explained in Vold and Bernard (1986). Although they focus particularly on conflict emerging from power differentials that define criminality, a factor considered in our approach to the definition of crime, we will be adding an analysis of the dynamics of interpersonal relations and the role social institutions play in controlling conflict derived from these interactions.

siveness in the family is associated with later aggressiveness outside the family.

> But when we look for evidence of a direct connection between broken and abusive homes and subsequent criminality, we find it is less clear cut than what we had supposed. The reason for this, we suggest, is that a broken or abusive home is only an imperfect indicator of the existence of a complex array of factors that contribute to criminality. (Wilson & Herrnstein, 1985:261)

According to this view, while abusive families can teach children to express their frustrations by resorting to violent action, the object of this violence can vary depending on other aspects of family experience and on the situation in which children find themselves. "Abused children may become tough soldiers instead of violent criminals, and of the latter, some will confine their violence to intimate settings and others will attack strangers" (Wilson & Herrnstein, 1985:261).

Wilson and Herrnstein (1985) argue that there is no social link between the violence in the family and the violence that is exhibited by individuals in criminal action. What they distill from their review of the literature is that the only real predictor of a progression to criminality is having the misfortune of lacking the constitutional traits to control impulsiveness, having an inadequate IQ, and relating to an unresponsive mother. The logical extension of this argument is that the violence encountered in the family is unimportant in modeling behavior relative to the role played by the genetic characteristics of an individual.

We find it difficult to discard the notion, as Wilson and Herrnstein do, that the ways in which interaction are carried out in the family will mold the ways in which people deal with problems in the future. This aspect of socialization goes beyond the statement of values—of what is right and wrong—and moves to the question of what, in practice, seems acceptable and what does not. The means of problem solving, the manner of dealing with conflict, and the procedures for handling frustration and violence are surely influenced by the role models that are provided in the family. Even more basic, the confrontations that currently take place between family members cannot be dismissed as unproblematic in their own right.

Wilson and Herrnstein (1985) pay little attention to the social contexts of the family that may have brought about an escalation to violence. They downplay the criminality that occurs in family violence with the new police mandates to arrest in those cases in which physical harm has occurred (Sherman & Berk, 1984). Wilson and Herrnstein are more concerned with whether or not an abusive home will produce children who will commit crime outside the home. This distinction between crime deriving from conflict in the home and crime that occurs outside the home is a spurious one.

The violence that emerges from domestic disputes seems to be poorly explained by heredity. The social contexts of family tension and the factors that escalate it to violence are relevant for consideration in any study of criminality, notwithstanding the effects that this violence may have in creating greater propensity to commit crimes in the future by its victims (Wilson & Herrnstein, 1985:253).

Surely the point that violence can occur in any context (whether as a soldier, a football player, or a criminal) only emphasizes the social acceptability of certain types of violence as opposed to those that are negatively sanctioned and punished. This view supports the perspective defined by Straus (1985) in his discussion of socially legitimate violence (see Chapter 1). Violence that is "acceptable" may easily become violence that is not. Wilson and Herrnstein (1985) ignore this transformation, thereby weakening the case they make concerning the propensity to criminality displayed by certain constitutionally defective individuals. Violent actions can be learned and may even be contagious (Nettler, 1984a:63). The learning process also applies, then, to the ways in which we handle conflict (including not handling it at all).

This point is illustrated by Hagan, who explains that much of the difference between male and female criminality may be a function of the different socialization and enforcement of laws for women versus men, not solely the constitutional differences between genders. With their greater involvement in the economic system of advanced capitalist societies, Hagan maintains, men have become more subject to formal social control in the emerging criminal justice system, whereas women are more influenced by the informal social control of the family. At the same time, men are the instruments of agencies of social control, whereas women have played the dominant role in socialization in the family (Hagan, 1986:78). Gender-based use of formal versus informal forms of social control brought' about through learning, then, has important implications for the ways in which we handle conflict.

The debate over genetic versus situational determinants of criminality has a parallel in the argument over the impact of personality versus situation in encouraging crime.

PERSONALITY VERSUS SOCIAL SITUATION IN GENERATING CONFLICT AND CRIME

Psychopathology versus Personal Frustration

On August 20, 1986, in Edmund, Oklahoma, Pat Sherill shot and killed 14 of his post office co-workers. He also wounded 6 others before killing himself. In their attempts to make sense of the killings, the media searched for clues in the events that led up to the murders. Sherill's fellow workers said they knew little about him, describing him as quiet and reserved. An assistant district attorney reported that Sherill apparently had no criminal record (*Globe and Mail*, 1986:A1–A2). The UPI report indicated that Sherill's neighbors saw him as unstable. They are quoted as saying that he hated dogs, he hated black people, he hated women, he hated his boss and his job, and he hated every job he had held since leaving the Marines (*Edmonton Sun*, 1986:2).

The picture painted by the press to explain the unexplainable was of a man out of control, just waiting to burst. But what triggered the final act? A clue to the explanation of the fatal outburst is provided by a report in the *New York Times* two days after the event. The *Times* reporter pointed to a negative job appraisal given to Sherill by his supervisor as a precipitating factor in the violence. The union steward at the post office was quoted as saying that managerial pressure could have played an important role in the slayings (*New York Times*, 1986b:12). The escalation of conflict between Sherill and post office officials was seen as a major reason for the violence.

Whether true or not, the need to find a rational explanation for what is seen by most people as irrational behavior makes us consider the role that day-to-day interpersonal conflict plays in enhancing or escalating violence. The image of the demented killer, randomly picking off victims, is more realistically replaced with a picture of an individual driven by stress who cannot control the conflict in his life. The escalation to violence occurs when problems are not mediated or resolved. What is noteworthy in the Sherill case and in other cases, such as that of James Huberty who shot 21 people at a McDonald's in San Ysidro, California, in 1984, is that he had no previous criminal record. In the Huberty case, as well, there had been repeated heated disputes with neighbors and employers (*Globe and Mail*, 1984a:A9).

Excessive violence deriving from frustration may explain the incidence of mass murders better than pathological explanations, according to Levin and Fox (1985). In their study of 364 cases of mass murder from 1976 through 1985 in the United States, they found that the common thread in behavior among murderers was severe frustration (Levin & Fox, 1985:68). Frustration appears as a precursor of a violent attack—a final straw. Usually, as in the Sherill case, there was some precipitating event. Further, the killer has few outside contacts with friends and neighbors who might help to reduce this growing rage. The implication in the research is that in those cases of mass murder in which the violence is most severe, uncontrolled conflict rather than psychopathology provides the best explanation of the final outcome.

The Sherill case illustrates the type of situation that fuels the debate over the importance of personality type versus social context in causing serious violence. On the one hand, it can be argued that the demented personality finds life too hard to manage and explodes in an inevitable outburst of rage and violence. On the other hand, many people who have violent dispositions are kept from endangering others by the constraints imposed by the social situation. In addressing this debate of personality versus social situation, psychologists have drawn from experimental analysis to identify the factors that elicit conflict between individuals and to suggest ways of diminishing this tension.

Conflict Style and Group Processes

To begin with, Sternberg and Soriano (1984) report that individual styles of handling conflict resolution vary across situations, suggesting the importance of personality in bringing people to these problems and helping them with solutions. They argue, consistent with the view expressed by Wilson and Herrnstein, that perception of the social circumstances surrounding the conflict is less important for resolution. In contrast, Mischel (1968) suggests that understanding personal behavior requires at least as much attention to the situation as to underlying personality dispositions. This view does not dismiss the role that personality plays in creating tension and friction between individuals. Research reported by Terhune (1970) suggests that conflict will be exacerbated by individuals with aggressive, dominant, dogmatic, and suspicious personalities. At the same time, he argues that these personal characteristics will be mitigated when participants are more likely to exhibit traits of egalitarianism, trust, and open-mindedness.

Stagner (1971) also disagrees with personality-based explanations of conflict. He states that perception of certain cues in social interaction will influence the ways in which the conflict is handled. In addition, beliefs, attitudes, and values will override personality to control conflict and resolve it (Deutsch, 1973). Situational factors play a role in reducing or, at least, containing the propensity to conflict and violence that derive from overly aggressive personalities. These cues may be a function of socialization. Jorgenson (1985) observes that generally siblings use a method of conflict resolution similar to the one used both between their parents and toward them.

In trying to untangle the situational versus personality aspects of conflict management, we may be able to see them as part of an interdependent whole (Kelley & Thibaut, 1978). The evolution of events occurs through the development of a **conflict style** applied by individuals in a manner consistent with their personality and appropriate to the social situation that they confront (Hocker & Wilmot, 1985:38). Hocker and Wilmot assume that people develop patterned responses to conflict that vary according to circumstance (indicating that personality may be less important than judgment in selecting a style). This decision about style is made on the basis of past experience and learning. People learn conflict styles by observing others' behavior and trying out different responses.

Coser (1956) states that the closer the relationship and the more that participants are involved in it, the more occasions there are for conflict. The more frequent the interaction, the more occasion for hostile interaction. Yet it is exactly the proximity of the relationship that leads people to avoid conflict in fear of permanently damaging the tie. Black (1980) makes the point that the sensitivity of the police to close social relationships leads them to be less likely to intervene. These relationships may actually contain greater levels of hostility and, therefore, greater possibility for violence. At the same time, if a relationship is stable, Coser points out that conflict allows for the immediate release of hostility so that it does not accumulate to the point where violent outbursts occur (Coser, 1956:83).

Realistic and Nonrealistic Conflict

The nature of conflict is governed, as well, by the rationality of the acts of the disputants. Realistic conflicts occur as a result of clashes of interests. They are limited in scope, however, as the struggle between disputants is only a means toward an end. If the desired result can be attained by any other means, these means may be employed. Conflict, then, is only one of several alternatives open to the individuals involved in the dispute (Coser, 1956:49). Nonrealistic conflict, however, arises exclusively as an aggressive impulse that seeks expression no matter what the object. "In such cases, no limitations exist, since it is not the attainment of the result, but rather the acting out of aggressive energies which occasions the outbreak" (Coser, 1956:49).

Turk (1966) discusses realistic and nonrealistic conflict in terms of crime. He states that we might assume that nonrealistic conflict is the product of pathology and realistic conflict comes from "normal" behavior. In fact, consistent with our discussion in Chapter 1, research has led to the realization that those things that are socially prized may be undesirable and those that are deviant may have their functions. The effect of the pathological motivation on creating nonrealistic conflict decreases as groups get larger. Thus not all conflict (nor crime) that seems aggressive, antagonistic, hostile, or irrational (i.e., nonrealistic) has to be a product of individual pathology. Rather this behavior may result from the passion or anger that emerges from a conflict in which the complexity of issues and factors in the environment lead to extreme reaction or unpredictable behavior. Conflict intensifies with depersonalization through the attachment of group interests to the dispute (Coser, 1956:115). An implicit "brinkmanship" occurs as a result of a conflict of this sort. Although personal disputes may be easily resolved, the pressure of the group may serve to extend group conflict and lead to more extreme measures in searching for a resolution. This perspective on realistic versus nonrealistic conflict emphasizes the relative importance of goal setting in relation to the level of rationality involved in the origins of conflict.

Conflict style, then, may be molded to conform to the demands of the group. Coser (1956) maintains that conflict may occur as a way of letting off steam, a "safety valve." The prospects of vengeance in interpersonal disputes play a role in escalating conflict. These are sometimes positively sanctioned, although our society is more likely to require that vengeance be meted out through formal agencies. When this vengeance is not taken or is inadequate, it is possible that people will engage in "self-help" (Black, 1983), taking steps to resolve the dispute themselves even if it may involve illegal behavior.

Reider (1984) indicates that self-help driven by vengeance may emerge despite the controlling elements of organized law. In fact, it is not unusual for the justice agencies themselves to resort to forms of ridicule and debasement of individuals as a form of revenge against the offenders' actions. The law may also tolerate vengeance that takes place outside of acceptable community standards in cases in which intimates are involved and there is a belief that retribution is the only form of resolution open to the victim. This community view of vengeance, however, is muted by popular repulsion toward emotional statements of revenge (see Jacoby, 1983).

Third Parties

As indicated in the research by Levin and Fox (1985), third parties can play an important role in reducing conflict. This reduction can be achieved through social cues and decision-making processes as major elements in lowering aggression and hostility and bringing about conciliation. The best way to bring about conflict resolution is through the development of structured decision making focused on specific issues (Donahue et al., 1985). For example, in reducing tension between neighborhood housing groups, Fisher and White (1976) apply mediation techniques. They conclude that there is value in using neutral third parties in developing programs of constructive confrontation in resolving conflict between public and private housing groups. Through this process, attitudes of antagonists will change, leading to more peaceful coexistence.

Fisher and White (1976) report that the process of third-party consultation has the desired effect when concerted efforts are made to articulate areas of tension and to deal with the complexity of problems. Psychologists and others have been sensitized to the idea that third-party intervention can be applied to conflict reduction through a learning process. The applied aspects of psychological study of conflict will be examined in greater detail in our review of mediation strategies in Chapter 5.

One of the more notable attempts at conflict resolution using a third-party approach was performed by Doob and Foltz (1973, 1974), who sought to bring together warring groups in Northern Ireland into a workshop that would promote cooperation and conciliation. Through a process of educating people in the workshop about the organization of groups, the sessions then focused on specific problems of dispute, including issues related to authority, power, and leadership. Added to this was discussion of specific instances of conflict and the ways in which they can be resolved. The workshop helped illustrate that the conflict in Northern Ireland not only is about justice but also is complicated by the problems of long-standing hatred set in a context of opportunities for violent actions (Doob & Foltz, 1973:511). The escalation to violence is made easier by the view that third-party means of dispute resolution of a nonviolent form are ineffective in bringing about peace. The importance of situation and tactics of peacemaking, then, overshadow the role that personality plays in these environments.

CRIMINAL PREDISPOSITION VERSUS GROUP PROCESSES

Strong versus Weak Social Ties

A great deal of research has been done on the importance of social ties for social well-being, establishing the fact that people are much more happy and feel less anomic when provided with informal social support (Unger & Wandersman, 1985). Without these ties, people will revert to social disorder and crime. The lack of commitment, attachment, or involvement will allow people to act out their worst scenarios on others (Hirschi, 1969). Added to this view is the observation that strong social ties with groups supporting conventional values (Hirschi's concept of belief) may be re-placed with ties to those who are deviant.

It has been argued that social ties with groups reinforcing conventional values can be weakened through high mobility and anonymity, which comes from living in densely populated and heterogeneous urban environments (Wirth, 1938). Wilson and Herrnstein (1985) dismiss these factors as having any measurable impact on criminality. Rather, they argue, it is the psychological isolation of compulsive individuals, unrestrained by group conventions, that leads to outbreaks of criminality.

Wilson extends this theme, pointing out that we have become accustomed to thinking of the law in essentially individualistic terms. "The law defines 'my' rights, punishes 'his' behavior, and is applied by 'that' officer because of 'this' harm" (Wilson, 1983:86). What is good for the individual, according to this thinking, is good for the community. This attitude causes problems when the reactions of others who are different from us (including fear, withdrawal, and flight) makes matters worse for everyone.

Krohn, Lanza-Kaduce, and Akers (1984) restate the case for the importance of weak versus strong ties in explaining deviance. Using conventional criminological theories, they put these explanations into the context of current experiences in North American cities. They argue that Wirth's (1938) and Fischer's (1975) different positions on the role of social relations in criminality share key components of two current theories: Hirschi's (1969) social bonding theory and Akers' (1977) social learning theory.

> While Wirth presented an image of the urban setting as disorganized, thus reducing constraints on residents and allowing for unpredictable behavior, Hirschi argued that deviant behavior is a result of the weakening or severing of one or more of the social bonds. Fischer's depictions of an integrated but highly diverse, urban setting is consistent with Akers' social learning theory, which emphasizes the learning of deviant behavior in (differential) association with others who provide models, definitions, and reinforcements for such behavior. (Krohn, Lanza-Kaduce, & Akers, 1984:355)

From the point of view of social bonding theory, the anonymity of city life creates weak social bonds, leading to increased deviance. However, it has been demonstrated, counter to Wirth's observations, that urban social ties are no fewer than rural ones (Fischer, 1975). Krohn and colleagues speculate that there is a difference instead in the quality of primary relationships across communities or that elements of the social bond differentiate between urban and rural areas, supporting a social learning approach to criminality. The differences in behavior come from differential contact with significant others in the environment. These individuals support or reduce the likely outbreak of social deviance.

Following this argument, Wolfgang and Ferracuti (1967) state that certain groups use violence as a means of continuous control over members. Research reported by Felson, Ribner, and Siegel (1984) reinforces the view that the presence of third parties will, in fact, escalate disputes to violence, and the possibility of resolution is enhanced when these individuals are absent. This strengthening of group ties through the advocacy of conflict makes individual attempts to seek resolution more difficult. The dynamics of the interpersonal dispute that occurs in groups may lead to important elements that fail to prevent the individual from pulling back from violence. With the promotion of the escalation of the violence, rather than an active search for solutions, by third parties added into the equation (Felson & Steadman, 1983), drastic measures may be chosen to end the dispute.

This promotion of violence may be situationally specific, however. As Hagan (1985) points out, there is no strong empirical evidence for the view that groups adhering to deviant subcultures promote violence, where violence is considered an integral aspect of the group's functioning. Could we conclude, instead, that there are no norms in these groups to deescalate violence once it begins? Here the emphasis is less on the promotion of conflict and more on its control,[2] a shift from subcultural explanation to one based on socialization.

The loss of social bonds derives from the segmented nature of social contacts that people experience in modern cities. What is evident, however, is that there is a two-step process that occurs in handling this social isolation. The breakdown of ties with significant others who may help to constrain deviant behavior can lead to socially isolated individuals looking for trouble. What is more likely is that these weak ties with family will be replaced by ties to friends. These groups may be less likely to be available to reduce the conflict that individuals experience, playing a less significant role in mediating their frustrations than is possible by people who are more intimate (Greider & Krannich, 1985). The segmentation in cities is cross-cut by cleavages that are based on ethnicity and socioeconomic background, where different backgrounds can lead to misunderstandings across groups, enhancing interpersonal conflict.

Racial and Ethnic Tensions

Following this theme of urban segmentation, Gordon (1985) presents a provocative new look at the factors in urban environments that have led to the decline of these areas and enhanced the degree to which they are experiencing crime. She says that the underlying social movements (or "plates") that are now operating in big cities arise from the problems that are encountered in Americans' inability to deal with racism. Difficulties emerge, as well, from their "cancerous individualism," short-term planning, and political nonaccountability. In addition, this individualism is derived from an inability to channel and interpret in a unified way the diversity of information and values that are transmitted through diverse channels of communication.

---

[2] This view is consistent with our discussion of third parties in the previous section.

The prominence of racial problems in inner cities leads to a surge away from these areas and into locations (e.g., suburbs) where these problems can be avoided or ignored. The pursuit of individual goals further justifies this flight. Both trends lead to a refusal to confront the inevitable conflict of divergent interests. They undermine the necessity to handle the unfortunate consequences of conflicts that emerge in urban areas from the frustration of poverty or the friction between racial or ethnic groups.

The conflict is left to those who have few resources to cope with it. This development is evident in neighborhoods where escape from racial tension in made difficult by low incomes or scarce affordable housing. Merry (1981), in her study of an urban area called Dover Square, focuses on the impact of "danger" on the day-to-day life of the inhabitants. She says that the notion of danger differs by ethnic group, as is illustrated by her description of the relationship between Blacks and Chinese.

> For example, the Chinese view of Blacks as dangerous and criminal is exacerbated by their belief that Blacks prey exclusively on them, while the Blacks' view of the Chinese as dangerous focuses on their hostile and suspicious attitudes, their reputed skill in the martial arts, and their implacable retaliation. (Merry, 1981:143)

This experience of racially based fear is not unique to the United States. Smith (1983) points out that many people in her studies of Birmingham, England, used ethnic stereotyping as a pragmatic means of managing the dangers of urban life. These informal strategies usually entail setting up social and physical distances in order to avoid potentially harmful encounters. This development is manifested in the evolution of "turf" in urban neighborhoods, sometimes patrolled by gangs of youths from different ethnic or racial backgrounds (Suttles, 1972). The conflict emerging in Los Angeles, depicted in the movie *Colors*, repeats a theme of gangs and urban territoriality presented in movies as diverse as *West Side Story* and *The Warriors*.

The role that crime plays in contributing to a sense of danger in cities shifts with the nature of intergroup conflict, based on stereotypes of the other group, that develops. Crime is compounded by interethnic and interracial slurs and degrading behavior. The confusion and misunderstandings that arise because of differences in family practices and cultural values further add to this problem.

It is obvious that these types of problems can escalate from insults to actual attack. Recently in Boston a random assault took place between Caucasian and Vietnamese youths over a traffic incident. It led to the death of one of the Vietnamese. These racially motivated, unprovoked attacks by strangers on individuals create the greatest fear among inner-city residents (Merry, 1981).

Social Status, Labels, and the Creation of Deviance

The problems of ethnic conflict are often confounded by stresses created by economic hardship. Socioeconomic status has been seen as a major social factor influencing the development of crime, differentiating groups according to inequality and unequal access to formal ways of resolving conflict (see, e.g., Taylor, Walton, & Young, 1973). Wilson and Herrnstein say, however, that there are contradictory findings on the effects of class on crime, which occur because there is no clear-cut agreement about how class is to be measured (Wilson & Herrnstein, 1985:28). The discussion of class-based crime allows only for the shift of blame from the individual to the society, thereby excusing this behavior or ignoring the psychogenetic basis of its origins. They propose to replace social class with other measures affecting social standing, such as schooling and labor market experiences.

Ignored by Wilson and Herrnstein (1985) are the different levels of conflict that occur across classes, contrasting availability of alternative informal means to resolve these conflicts, varying access to resources to pursue formal complaints, and different responses on the part of the criminal justice system to class-based conflict.[3] That these class-related phenomena have consequences for the level of criminality is hard to dispute. Whether social class directly creates criminality is a much more complicated question.

One approach to the incorporation of class-based explanations is criminology has been proposed by labeling theorists. Labeling (or "societal reaction") theory argues that the agencies of social control create deviance through their *overcontrol* of individual behavior based on stereotypes and negative reactions to members of a social "underclass" (Hagan, 1985). This view extends the idea of an overreach of the law, discussed in Chapter 1, to include an explanation based on class.

The police, it is argued, impose criminal labels on those individuals who assume characteristics of offenders. Labeling theory narrows definitions of crime to the reactions of individuals, turning attention away from the basic conflict that they experience. The definition process has been described as follows:

> Court hearings, home investigations by social workers, arrests, clinical visits, segregation within the school system and the formal dispositions of

---

[3] These are questions that will be addressed in some detail in Chapters 5 and 7.

deviants under the aegis of public welfare or public protection in many instances are cause for dramatic redefinitions of the self and role of deviants which may or may not be desired. (Lemert, 1951:70–71)

Labeling theorists believe that deviants become defined as such through a process of stigma, degradation, and stereotyping. The social control agencies, including police, courts, and prisons, segregate those individuals described as deviant. They promote, through this action, further deviance. Individuals with certain labels are more likely to become "victims" of the bureaucratic machinery of control agencies. This explanation moves the causation, then, from what we do to who we are (Nettler, 1984a:265).

Labeling ignores the fact that there is a process through which criminality can be defined and redefined according to circumstance or interest. What is of note is that Lemert, an important proponent of labeling, began his investigation of deviance with a focus on conflict. In Lemert's terms, the situation in which deviation is present is *structured in conflict terms and values*. What this leads to is an amplification of the societal reaction to this deviance (Lemert, 1951:56). This theory presumes deviance as a factor separate from and in existence prior to conflict. It is with this point that we would disagree most strongly with the labeling theorists. We would argue instead that conflict is a precursor of deviance, with the definition of deviance emerging from rather than being exacerbated by the conflict process.

This change in emphasis is consistent with the previous criticisms that we must set crime into the context of the social structure to better understand its origins and development. More important, we derive from this perspective a view of crime as negotiated rather than predetermined. We respond to crime in a mediative way so it makes sense to define it in these terms. The focus on defining criminals according to our reactions to them presents a single-sided view of how criminalization takes place. It seems clear now that labeling theory is inadequate in its conceptualization of individual offenders as victims of the system of social control. Although it does bring attention to the interchange that occurs between individuals and social agencies, it dismisses the possibility that a great deal of this interaction can take place without the imposition of such labels.

Further, Scull says that almost exclusive attention to the impact of organizations on the individual results in only cursory attention being paid to the structure of these organizations themselves. It also neglects the overarching structural context within which particular agencies of social control operate (Scull, 1984:10). Further, the actions of social control agencies are seen to be arbitrary, determined simply by the immediate interests of the first-line controllers (e.g., police). Scull points out that the ritual acknowledgment that those who label (or who construct and impose new labels) are more powerful than those who are labeled represents a dismal substitute for the analyses of the power structure and its impact (Scull, 1984:11). We will address the role of social control agents in defining and reacting to crime when we discuss the police in Chapter 6.

So although we disagree with Wilson and Herrnstein (1985) that class is unimportant in explaining variations in criminality, it is too simplistic to argue that crime results simply from shifting the blame from society to the individual through the imposition of criminal labels. The conflict that emerges from power differentials based on class appears to provide a more useful base for understanding the origins of crime and the response of social control agencies to it.

SUMMARY

We have seen in this chapter that conflict-based crime can be studied from many different angles. Informal mechanisms for handling conflict provide a means for identifying the impact of psychological versus social situational factors in promoting conflict. These pressures are mediated by the presence of third parties and can be influenced by the perceptions of the actors concerning the success of certain styles of conflict resolution that they may need to adopt.

The adherence of individuals to groups shows that conflict has important social roots. Group action also influences the management of hostility and revenge. It may enhance perceptions of enemies and change one's view of the acceptability of certain behavior in dealing with these individuals. In reviewing the discussion of conflict, we see that there is an easy route to explaining it in terms of individual deviation, defining it as irrational and psychopathic, a result of problems of undersocialization. This direct channel from individual deviation based on constitutional defects to crime leaves us with a sense that this behavior is predetermined. Punishment and restraint, then, are really the only options available to us to reduce criminality.

The targeting of individuals as constitutionally deficient may be suitable for definitions of aggressiveness or violence. But it is the second person in the role as catalyst and the presence of third persons in conflicts that draw out the conflict or control it. Richard Gelles[4] talks about the excuses that wife batterers give when confronted in counseling sessions about their behavior. They say in their defense that they didn't know what they were doing, most often because they beat their wives when blind drunk. Gelles responds to this argument simply by asking the batterers why

---

[4] Personal communication.

they didn't keep beating their wives until they killed them. Something was there to regulate the behavior, even when let loose in the anger and blindness of family confrontations.

Conflict can be exacerbated, as well as controlled, by the cleavages that appear in society based on ethnic and socioeconomic standing. The power differentials in managing society's resources in defining and controlling social conflict can play an important role in which crime comes to be dealt with as a social problem. Although personality and predispositions to act may serve as factors in promoting the escalation to crime, the conditioning effects of social forces must be considered in any explanation of the origins of criminal behavior.

CHAPTER 3

The Origins of Social Conflict: Dispute Careers and Their Relationship to Crime

INTRODUCTION

In a well-publicized case in 1985, two men who had been feuding for years ended their disagreement one day by shooting one another in a parking lot. This case brought to public attention the desperation that can emerge from social conflict regularly encountered in today's society (*People*, 1985). The dispute originated with a lawsuit over the ownership of cattle and then escalated into a series of violent acts. These included bombings and shootings. Throughout a three-year period the two men taunted and ridiculed each other. According to the story, there was no definable reason for the deaths to have happened on the day they did.

The deaths left the families and friends of these men in a quandary over why the situation got out of hand. When the sheriff of the town was interviewed, he blamed the law for being so bogged down with technicalities. Nobody, he argued, has the chance to solve their problems anymore. He added that equally at fault was the unwillingness of the men to file formal complaints against one another. Ironically, both thought that this would simply make the situation worse.

In summarizing the events that led up to the shootings, the sheriff suggested that country people tend to be self-reliant and are less likely to seek help from others (*People*, 1985:91). Surely, this last statement contradicts the widespread belief that people in rural areas make use of informal means for resolving disputes, which is why the formal avenues are less often used. Yet these two men chose to resolve their dispute in their own way—terminally. Neither family nor friends sought to deescalate the dispute, or if they did, they did not convince the two men that there was an alternative to their final solution.

The evidence is clear that homicides, although they occur infrequently, are most often preceded by interpersonal conflict. Close to three-quarters of the murders committed in Canada in the last 25 years (about 7,500 cases in which a motive was assigned) were a result of revenge, jealousy, anger, or argument. Only about 15 percent were preceded by another crime or a sexual assault (Silverman & Kennedy, 1988). This record demonstrates the importance of conflict management in keeping disputes from getting out of control and becoming lethal.

The escalation of the feud, and its resolution through violence underline the view expressed by Nader and Singer (1976:262) that the formal approach of legal sanctions and punishment has left much conflict in society submerged from public view, coming to prominence only when it escalates to violence and crime. The conflict that exists may not be dealt with by formal agencies because of their inability to handle any other than the most serious offenses. Thus much conflict that is harmful to individuals may remain untreated, a notable case being the problems encountered in family violence. However, as pointed out earlier, the unreported crimes that come from interpersonal conflict are unreported or untreated because of the reluctance of the individuals involved to go beyond their informal solutions. They use their own resources to bring about a solution (Kennedy, 1988).

The ways in which disputes are handled in contemporary society will provide the focus of this chapter. We have seen in the previous chapters that conflict has many forms and many different origins. The process by which interpersonal conflict is defined as a dispute, expands or contracts, and becomes resolved will now be analyzed.

DISPUTE PYRAMIDS AND THE DISPUTE CAREER

There is a widespread popular belief that Americans are overly litigious, taking all their grievances to formal adjudication through the courts. Galanter (1983) says that there is continued debate about this "hyperlexis explosion," or overuse of the courts. He finds no evidence that hyperlexis is as prominent as commonly believed, despite the great number of disputes that occur in society on a daily basis.

> Disputes are drawn from a vast sea of events, encounters, collisions, rivalries, disappointments, discomforts, and injuries. . . . Some things in this sea of "proto-disputes" become disputes through a process in which

injuries are perceived, persons or institutions responsible for remedying them are identified, forums for presenting these claims are located and approached, claims are formulated acceptably to the forum, appropriate resources are invested, and attempts at diversion resisted. (Galanter, 1983:12)

The disputes that ultimately arrive at court are few and are the survivors of a long and selective process. Galanter suggests a "dispute pyramid" in which a large number of conflicts occur at the bottom. Those that reach litigation are the few on the top. This pyramid is not static because changes in perceptions of what is harmful in the social structure and in economic relations can alter attributions of responsibility and expectations of redress (Galanter, 1983:18). The operation of the dispute pyramid can be influenced by the ways in which disputes are transformed and redefined through their "careers" (Gulliver, 1979; Nader & Todd, 1978).

The knowledge of law and the skill in manipulating it can become critical resources for defining and transforming disputes. This use of law can be further confounded by the nature of the adversarial system, which encourages definitions of disputes in which there are only winners and losers and nothing in between (Miller & Sarat, 1980–81). Seeing disputes as having careers typifies the standard definition of civil suits (Christie, 1986). The dispute career begins with individuals perceiving an injustice. This perception leads to conflict, in which one individual confronts another with a claim of injustice. Individuals can then go public with the problem and seek out a third party to help in dealing with the conflict (Nader & Todd, 1978). Dispute careers are constrained by the norms of the society that dictate the rules of resolution. These can include the use of informal sanction and control.

The development of the dispute career assumes that individuals recognize the injustice perpetrated on them and plan to do something about it. **Naming, blaming,** and **claiming** are the steps that Felstiner, Abel, and Sarat (1980–81) identify as characterizing this process. The first step, **naming,** involves saying to oneself that a particular experience has been injurious. The naming of the experience transforms a normal interaction into a dispute. For example, whereas one might consider that name calling in an argument may not constitute a problem, it becomes injurious if one party believes that the name calling is defamatory because others might believe the slander.

The next step, **blaming,** involves attributing the injury suffered to the fault of another individual or social entity. "This definition takes the grievant's perspective: the injured person must feel wronged and believe that something might be done in response to the injury, however politically or sociologically improbable such a response might be" (Felstiner, Abel, &

Sarat, 1980–81:635). In the blaming step, using the name-calling example, the injured party would threaten to sue for slander.

The third transformation, **claiming**, occurs when the grievant confronts the person or entity believed to be responsible and asks for some remedy. In the claiming stage the injured party would document the injury due to the name calling and demand compensation, either through an apology or money. If it is not forthcoming, the recourse may be a more formal claim through the courts.

It is possible that the grievant may "claim" through self-help; that is, the grievance is resolved through criminal action. A grievance based on a criminal act can be resolved through informal means by the two parties. Whether people perceive an experience as an injury, blame someone else, claim redress, or have their claims accepted depends on their social position, as well as their individual characteristics.

DEFINING DISPUTE PROCESSES

The Language of Disputes

In the evolution of the dispute through naming, blaming, and claiming, the focus of the dispute becomes more defined through a narrowing of the issues (Mather & Yngvesson, 1980–81). In the process, established categories are used to organize the issues and events in the dispute. Which category will be used is of considerable significance to the outcome of the dispute. Disputes will narrow in ways acceptable to a third party (either by appealing to the third party's judgment or having this definition imposed). This view complements our review of the theories of crime presented in Chapter 2, with its emphasis on the social contexts of crime and the role of third parties in defining criminality. The dispute forms a basic unit in our examination of the conflict basis of crime. Three elements can affect this narrowing process: language, audience, and participants (Mather & Yngvesson, 1980–81).

Language is used to define a dispute. The conflict becomes a social construct in which "facts" are ordered and "norms" invoked in particular ways—"ways that reflect the personal interests or values of the participant or that anticipate the definitions offered by others" (Mather & Yngvesson, 1980–81:780). Understanding the language of disputes is most critical in situations in which legal codes and legal discourse are employed.

Mather and Yngvesson's (1980–81) report on literature shows that the subculture of the criminal court routinely modifies the categories of crime to produce working definitions of "normal crime" and "real criminals." Interestingly enough, the categorization of cases within the adult criminal court generally suggests a higher tolerance for deviance than that found in the general society. Black (1983:39) reinforces this point when he discusses criminal cases arising from quarrels and fights, where each party has a grievance against the other. The state imposes the categories of offender and victim on people who are contesting the proper application of these labels during the altercation.

Further, because of the dichotomized nature of criminal law, acts become right or wrong (noncrimes or crimes) and persons become criminals or noncriminals (Christie, 1986:96). Fundamentally, penal law looks more into acts than into interactions—which removes the negotiated feature of civil disputes from penal or criminal ones. Claiming becomes a process of defining an offender and a victim. But this transformation of the dispute does not deny its origins in conflict or the negotiation over punishment that occurs after the criminality is established.

The narrowing and expanding of disputes is dependent, then, on language that defines the grievance and categorizes the nature of the conflict. There is an important insight here, especially when we consider this problem in the context of definitions of crime and the role that disputes have in affecting the evolution to crime. There may, in fact, not be a change in the behavior. Rather a judgment can be made that the dispute will best be dealt with as criminal through a narrowing process. Alternatively, a criminal act may be expanded to illustrate the grievance of the actors and justified in terms of saving property, face, or principle.

Through plea negotiation, this definition may change further to accommodate court definitions (Mather & Yngvesson, 1981:794). Plea bargaining is a form of negotiation in the court.[1] But as Strauss (1978) points out, implicit negotiations are a constant part of any social order. It is conceivable that the very process of disputing involves some sort of plea bargaining in the stages in which the dispute is still outside of the formal court process:

> ...reaching such understanding and making such tacit agreements do not occur in a social order vacuum; they occur against a backdrop of explicit agreements (some of them negotiated) reached in the distant or recent past, as well as (family) rules that for some (family members) may have been partially negotiated as well as imposed from above. Of course, in both formal organizations and families, there may be coercive relations that are very much a part of the structural context that pertains to both implicit and explicit negotiating. For both kinds of negotiating, a social order is necessary. (Strauss, 1978:225)

---

[1] We discuss plea bargaining in Chapter 7.

It is the process of negotiation that brings about this social order, which in Strauss' terms has been ignored in the social science literature.

Audience and the Redefinition of Disputes

Audience participation can vary from virtual exclusion of anyone but the participants to direct involvement by outsiders watching the process, following its progress, or verbally engaging in the ongoing discussions (Mather & Yngvesson, 1980–81:782). As discussed in Chapter 2, the audience can affect the intensity of the dispute, as is illustrated by the research of Felson and Steadman (1983). They suggest that criminal violence may follow systematic patterns in situations in which this violence is not committed in conjunction with other crimes. This violence begins with attacks on one another's identity through insults, rejection, accusation, complaints, and physical violence not involving actual harm (e.g., pushing). There may also be an attempt to influence a third party. The identity attacks and noncompliance may lead to threats and evasive action. The attempt to confront or avoid the situation and the antagonist involves a possibility that retaliation may occur. An aggressive action in defense of one's identity may prompt an equally aggressive response. It is in these cases that weapons often appear and people are killed.

Felson and Steadman state that the picture that emerges is not one of blindly irrational behavior. Rather, each participant's actions are a function of the other person's behavior and the implication of that action for defending one's own well-being and one's honor. The victims, it is also noted, are aggressive and are at least partially responsible for the outcome (Felson & Steadman, 1983:73).

Expanding the dispute changes the perspective from which the third party ordinarily views the act, person, or relationship involved in the conflict by placing it in new context.

> ...individuals and groups have vested interests in particular definitions of persons and events; changes in definitions tend to meet with resistance, and thus require some basis of support if they are to succeed...the new labels act as a catalyst in their shaping of perception. (Mather & Yngvesson, 1980–81:799)

This expansion can occur because of the role played by a third party in the dispute (e.g., mediator or judge), because of action by supporters who want to expand a dispute to a fight on a principle, or through the actions of an audience (such as a relevant peer group, who although not a party to the dispute, is affected by its outcome).

In sum, disputes may expand when an organizational framework is imposed on the events and the relationships encompassed by the dispute. "The consequences of dispute expansion may be limited to the dispute itself or they may involve broad legal or political change" (Mather & Yngvesson, 1980–81:798). Factors that would help explain the outcome and consequences of expansion include degree of dissatisfaction (both in intensity and scope) with the established order in society; extent to which those who are unhappy with the established order for reasons of their own would benefit from an ordering of issues along the lines suggested in the expansion; timing of emergence of a particular case in relation to other similar ones; particular constellation of facts and issues on the case itself; relation of redefinition to parallel political cleavages; and extent to which an audience becomes involved in the disputing process, giving credibility and support to the shift in perspectives (Mather & Yngvesson, 1980–81:798).

If we consider these issues in the context of landlord–tenant relations, for example, the conflict that develops over specific problems related to rent or the quality of maintenance of the dwelling may broaden to include other types of issues. The tenants may group together to form a political union to force local government to clamp down on landlords and enact stronger laws to restrict rent gouging or conversions to condominiums. These tenant groups may actually expand to become legitimate political interests, finding, through their combined power, the ability to influence courts to accept their positions in conflicts with landlords.

Participant Characteristics and the Dispute Career

Participants to disputes vary in their power to shape the dispute and influence the outcome. This power can be affected by the degree of knowledge of the legal process, experience, economic resources, or social standing (Turk, 1976). We will examine the importance of such additional factors as socioeconomic status and ethnicity in the use of mediation programs and the general access to courts in Chapters 5 and 7.

Social context can also affect individual choice of resolution. Felstiner (1974) argues that the lack of group support in technological societies leads to individuals having no recourse if the formal agencies are unable or unwilling to deal with their problem. Informal or group-based coercion has little impact on bringing about conformity, he states. Avoidance, then, is the result. But if people cannot find support in formal or informal agencies, surely then Black (1983) is correct in his argument that people will turn instead to self-help by taking the resolution of the problem into their own hands. Equally valid is the assumption that there will be much unreported and unresolved crime.

To understand the process of dispute management, we can examine empirical data collected on the ways in which individuals deal with conflict and how it is affected by their relationship to others in the dispute, their use of others in solving these problems, and their satisfaction with the outcome of this process of resolution.

DISPUTE PROCESSING: AN EMPIRICAL TEST

The Study

The principles of dispute processing can be examined in greater detail through an assessment of survey data. The study presented here was designed to identify the ways in which people resolve disputes and who they use to help them in this process. This analysis focuses on three different types of disputes (Merry, 1979): property and crime-initiated disputes, neighborhood social order problems, and interpersonal conflicts.

Merry (1979) reports that crime-initiated disputes, including violent attacks and threats against the person, occur between acquaintances. She found that these types of disputes were usually dealt with through the police or the direct use of violence. Neighborhood disputes erupt over physical and social order. From Merry's research, these disputes occur between people who are acquainted but are not friends and do not share a similar culture or life style. Problems often go on for a long time and are fought out bitterly between the people who enter into the disagreement. The third type of dispute, the interpersonal conflict, relates to breaches in ongoing relationships, which may include personal rivalry or insult. We can add to this list disputes that occur because of misunderstandings or because of one party reneging on an agreement with another, including debts.

The results reported here are drawn from the 1984 and 1985 Edmonton Area Studies, the eighth and ninth in a series of annual surveys conducted by the Population Research Laboratory at the University of Alberta (Kinzel, 1985). The survey questionnaires, administered to cross-sectional samples of the residents of the City of Edmonton, involved one-hour structured interviews.[2] What is examined in this research includes measures of whether or not disputes of different types had been resolved

---

[2] Recent municipal records were used to generate a simple random sample of 560 addresses in 1984 and 545 in 1985. In family households chosen, either the husband or wife was eligible for interviewing. In nonfamily households (i.e., any person or group of nonrelated persons occupying a dwelling), any member over 18 years of age was eligible. The final response rate in 1984 was 80.7 percent and in 1985 it was 77 percent. In 1984, 51 percent of the final respondents were male and 49 percent were female. The median age of the sample was 34. In 1985, 47 percent were male and 53 percent were female. The median age in 1985 was 39 (Kinzel, 1985).

by the respondents. They were asked if they had been involved in any of the following disputes in the previous three years: (a) someone refused to pay money that was owed; (b) someone in the neighborhood was causing the respondent problems or being a nuisance (e.g., making noise late at night); (c) someone threatened to harm the respondent physically; (d) someone physically attacked the respondent or took something from the respondent by force.

Those who had been in disputes were asked whether or not they had been able to find a solution to their conflict. The response categories were yes (1) and no (2). The questions on the resolution of the disputes relating to physical attack and threat parallel Merry's categories of criminal disputes. Money disputes are typical of Merry's interpersonal conflicts.

Figure 3.1 outlines the stages in dispute resolution. We began with identifying the type of dispute and whether or not individuals had been involved in it in the previous three years. This represents the **naming** phase of the dispute career. The **blaming** process involves identifying who was involved in the dispute; were they family, relatives, neighbors, or strangers? Finally, how was the **claim** made? Was the dispute resolved, and if it was, who resolved it? The third parties involved in bringing about a resolution could have been friends or relatives or formal agencies such as landlords, the police, or the courts. Alternatively, the respondents may have simply dealt with the disputes themselves. How the conflict was re-solved could have included avoidance, confrontation, or mediation through informal means or arbitration through the courts. The level of satisfaction with the resolution then ended the inquiry. This model of the dispute career addresses the treatment of different types of conflict and the role that outside groups and agencies play in bringing about resolution.

Findings Related to Disputes

Two crime-based disputes were included in the analysis: physical threat and physical attack. Twelve percent reported receiving a physical threat in the last three years. This threat most often originated with strangers (45.9%), rather than friends (14.7%) and acquaintances (24.8%). In 75.2 percent of the cases, the threat disputes were resolved, most often by the respondent (49.4%). Police were sometimes involved (21.5%) but rarely did these threats make their way into court (5.1%).

Disputes deriving from physical threat were resolved through con-frontation, not avoidance. People most often talked their way out of the dispute (23.7%) or used force or yelling (31.3%). Avoidance was used 18.8 percent of the time, and police were called in 13.7 percent of the cases. In 12.5 percent, a court sentence was involved. Eighty-eight percent of the respondents expressed satisfaction with the outcome. It is surprising how

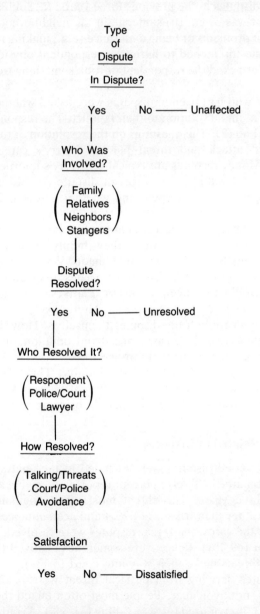

Figure 3.1. Stages in Dispute Resolution

rarely the police were called to deal with these problems even when strangers made up a large proportion of those who issued threats. When police were called, based on the low-level use of the courts, it would appear that they rarely charged anyone.

Of 873 respondents, 5.8 percent were physically attacked or someone took something from them by force. In 51 percent of these cases, a stranger was involved. In over half of all cases (66.7%), the dispute was resolved. Surprisingly, the strategy chosen most often was to deal with the problem oneself (58.8%). The second most used strategy was to call the police (29.4%). What is not so consistent is how the attack was resolved. The solutions included violence or yelling (35.4%), leaving the danger area (9.6%), or discussing the dispute (9.6%). Police or courts were used to resolve a minority of cases (12.9%). Most respondents expressed satisfaction (75.8%) with the resolution.

Although Black (1980) argues that police are more likely to arrest in disputes between strangers, the extent of such conflicts that can be defined as criminal but do not come to the attention of the police may be considerable. This underreporting, furthermore, may be due to the fact that the aftermath of the physical attack includes a resolution of the problem that is satisfactory to both sides and does not leave a victim with recourse only through the courts.

Thirty percent of the respondents had been involved in a neighborhood dispute. Of these, 80.5 percent involved neighbors, although strangers were also involved 14.1 percent of the time. In the majority of these disputes, there was resolution (68.3%), often through the action of the respondent (24%). It was in these situations that people made use of the police (22.3%) and landlords (17.9%). This high use of formal means of resolving neighborhood disputes is in contrast with the suggestion by Felstiner (1974) that people will use avoidance instead of confrontation. Although this strategy is adopted by some (about 40%), most people use other resources to deal with a problem. This strategy seems to lead, in most cases (92.1%), to a satisfactory solution.

Another common form of dispute is one involving money. Approximately one-quarter of the respondents had been involved in this form of dispute, most often with friends (39.4%) and acquaintances (20.4%). Frequently (67.6%) there was no resolution. When there was resolution, it was most often the respondent who brought it about (50%). Occasionally, a lawyer was brought in resolve the dispute (18.2%). The tactic most often used was to talk out the problem with the other person (72.1%), although sometimes threats and confrontation were necessary. The respondents seemed happy with the resolution (85.5%). Money problems can be a source of great conflict, and yet respondents preferred to handle these disputes on their own.

Relationship in Resolving the Dispute

Relationship may affect how disputes are resolved. Of all disputes, the two types in which there is a significant relationship between relational distance and resolution strategies are physical threat and physical attack. When we examined physical threat we found that for family members two different responses were used. A third of the respondents reported resolving problems with other family members by talking them out, whereas a surprising 42 percent claimed that these threats were resolved through court sentencing. Probably the latter were interspousal disputes, which have been increasingly finding their way into court because of changes in public attitudes toward police intervention in this area (Dutton, 1988).

The threatening behavior of friends and strangers was treated quite differently. Most often, friends talked out their problems (34.4%) but these disputes could also lead to force and yelling (31.3%). Police and courts were rarely used (15%). With strangers, it was force and yelling (40%), as well as avoidance (25.7%), which made up the major response to threats.

Relationship, then, seems to have an inverse effect on resolving threatening behavior. There was greater avoidance with strangers and greater involvement of formal justice agents with intimates. These findings bring new light to the view (Black, 1980) that the police are less prone to become involved in disputes between intimates. What is evident, however, is that very few threatening disputes came to their attention in the first place (less than 25%).

Looking at attack disputes, we found a similar pattern of higher use of police and courts when intimates were involved (60%). What is surprising in these results is that for both family and strangers, there was considerable use of violent response to attacks (40% and 50%, respectively). The inclination of individuals to use self-help may arise from suspicion of or reluctance to use the police. However, it also may be that the conditions of the dispute are such that individual action is the most appropriate at the time. When retribution is obtained on the spot, there may be no more need to seek out formal justice. This form of resolution may be unsettling to many, but the extent to which it is used raises the question of whether or not people will voluntarily move away from this strategy.

A caution raised by Kidder (1983) returns to the point made by Turk (1976) that we cannot assume that all disputes occur between people of equal resources or power. The protection of individuals who find themselves confronted by threat or attack in situations where they cannot hope to defend themselves is an integral element of our criminal justice system. Future work on self-help will have to deal with this problem in some detail.

MYTHS ABOUT DISPUTES AND DISPUTING

We can summarize the different aspects of disputes by addressing them in the context of myths that have developed to characterize the way conflict is handled in modern society. Cain and Kulscar (1981–82), in reviewing the current beliefs about disputes, are critical of the fact that researchers have focused on the part that social relations play in the disputing process rather than the part that conflict plays in social relations. This distinction presses home the view that the dispute, not unlike criminality, has typically been studied outside of the context of social reality.

The first myth is that disputes are universal. However, there is disagreement over the assumption that similar disputes appear consistently in all societies and that similar tactics can be applied in their resolution. Gulliver (1979) argues that dispute processing is basically similar across all cultures. Cain and Kulscar (1981–82) disagree, maintaining that qualitative differences emerge across societies according to social structure, government, and custom.

The second myth is that "ideological functionalism" promotes the *need* to bring about resolution of disputes. "Society is by definition ordered; a dispute is a moment of disorder; it is therefore unthinkable as a permanent condition" (Cain & Kulscar, 1981–82:379). The thought that by removing disputes we can restore order is similar to the belief that by eradicating crime we can regain order. The demand for the resolution of disputes should not preempt an unbiased view of the function that conflict (and especially disputes) plays in the ongoing social process.

Third, there is a presumption that courts should settle all disputes, with the corollary that if they do not or cannot, alternative institutions should be established to do so (Cain & Kulscar, 1981–82:379). In fact, with the exception of marital matters, a large number of interpersonal disputes are not dealt with in the courts (Cain & Kulscar, 1981–82: 387). This fact may mean that people are not adequately dealing with their conflicts or it may mean that they have determined that they can solve their difficulties without the use of court facilities. Galanter has determined that only a small proportion of troubles and injuries become disputes, with a small number of these becoming lawsuits. Of those that do go to litigation, the vast majority are abandoned, settled, or routinely processed without full-blown adjudication (Galanter, 1983). These relationships are substantiated in the research reported above.

Christie (1977) makes the point, following the logic from Nader and Singer (1976), that there are, in fact, too few conflicts in society, partly because they are assumed as property by the lawyers and other professionals tied into the criminal justice system. That is, conflicts are transformed by these professionals into nonconflicts. They are handed back to the disputants as resolved when in fact this does not meet the disputants' needs. The disputants have little chance to participate in the actual deliberation or resolution of the conflict. The professionals take over this task. The depersonalization and segmentation of society ensure even more that this professionalization is dominant and that bureaucratic solutions, for better or worse, are provided to the disputants (Aubert, 1967). This process may ensure due process and equitable outcomes, but as Christie points out, it also deprives individuals of the opportunity to follow the different stages of their conflict, ensuring a solution that fits their own circumstances.

Thus according to Cain and Kulscar (1981–82), using the single term *dispute* to encompass all matters of conflict is likely to lead to false theorization about the courts and to misdirected attempts at reform. This problem is especially of concern in the context of court capacity, negotiation strategies in courts, and equal access to justice. There are, as well, important implications for the ways in which formal justice relates to informal practice. For example, the preclusion of self-help in resolving disputes may mean frustration and aggravation deriving from the continuation of a dispute that has not reached the court but cannot be solved through individual initiative.

The fourth myth is an assumption in the literature that it would be simple to redistribute power to all individuals, ensuring fair and just solutions to conflict. This belief ignores the dimensions of social structure and political influence, which combine to affect access to power. It is not enough, in other words, to make institutions fairer in their judgments. One must also consider the values and roles that the individuals themselves bring to the dispute, which are important in affecting how it will be resolved.

Along this line, Cain and Kulscar (1981–82) go so far as to argue that class conflicts cannot be seen as disputes at all because they have their roots in larger political, economic, and social forces in the society. It seems extreme, though, to discard those disputes that occur on the community level. There is a need to understand the elements of community structure that impinge on personal relations, which contribute to the dispute process.

Fifth, related to the myth of universality is the view that there is a comparability in the response to disputes. This belief in comparability has led to strong arguments for the transferability of institutions that work to mediate disputes in other societies to a North American context, where these mechanisms have been slow to develop naturally in the social environment. This argument has found supporters and detractors (see specifically the debate over community mediation between Felstiner, 1975, and Danzig & Lowy, 1975, discussed in Chapter 5).

From Cain and Kulscar's point of view, one can pick up ideas from any source, but one cannot transport institutions and practices between societies with different modes of production (e.g., socialist versus capitalist) without bringing about a change in the political and ideological structures of the recipient society (Cain & Kulscar, 1981–82:390). Whether or not we agree on the need to change society to accommodate transfers of conflict management, we can agree that we must be aware of the origin of these alternative forms to understand the degree to which they work or fail in their application to our society.

This discussion sets the stage for an examination of how we have responded, through law and corrections, to social conflict and crime. The role that disputes play in setting a background for criminality must be accounted for in our responses to social disorder. Reducing undesirable behavior through deterrence and punishment is contingent on applying broad terms of reference that include informal, as well as formal, constraints. These issues will be reviewed in Chapter 4.

SUMMARY

The dispute pyramid depicts the large number of conflicts in our society. We see that only a few reach litigation. The emergence of disputes can be influenced by a number of social factors, which create pressures for narrowing and expanding the careers of these conflicts. Dispute careers go through distinct stages, including naming, blaming, and claiming. Important in maintaining a dispute career are language, participants, and audience. These can influence the growth or disappearance of a dispute and affect whether or not they come to be dealt with by the criminal justice system.

In an examination of data from a combined sample of two cross-sectional surveys, we find that the dispute career varies according to the type of conflict that is encountered. Crime-based disputes are most often between strangers. They are, despite this fact, most often dealt with by the respondent. Police find their way into physical threat or attack disputes rarely if they are between strangers and more often if they are between intimates. Generally, however, the police are not even informed of these disputes.

In neighborhood disputes, police are more likely to be used, as are landlords, for resolving problems. There is, at the same time, a fair amount of avoidance. Finally, in interpersonal disputes around money, there is low likelihood of success in solving the problem. It rarely goes beyond individual self-action.

These findings are important in judging the extent to which our counts of crime and court use truly reflect the criminal problem. This is not simply another question raised about hidden crime or victimization, but it involves definitions of crime originating from disputes and the situations conducive to these disputes.

Are there thresholds that people pass over before they decide to include the formal agencies in the dispute? Merry (1979) suggests that thresholds are culturally based and may arise as a consequence of confrontation between heterogeneous groups living in one neighborhood. More attention should be given to the conditions in communities that set the context for the development, evolution, and conclusion of disputes. With this information, we may be better able to understand, if not prevent, the escalation of interpersonal disputes to the point at which they seem resolvable only through extreme violence, such as two people shooting one another in a parking lot.

CHAPTER 4

Legal Responses to Crime and Conflict

INTRODUCTION

Sutherland argues that crime is itself conflict, which emerges when a certain group of people feels that its values are endangered by the behavior of others. Responding to this conflict through the imposition of law defines criminality. As Sutherland maintains, if the group is politically influential, its values important, and the danger serious, it will secure the enforcement of law, winning the cooperation of the state in the effort to protect its values (Sutherland, 1929:41).

Related to the implementation of law is the enactment of punishment. Sutherland indicates that there had been, in the early part of this century, a decline in the use of punishment. He says, though, that there are conflicting sentiments expressed about the usefulness of punishment in deterring future criminals. Sutherland indicates that the confusion over punishment comes from the fact that it can be demonstrated to have two effects. Sometimes it develops respect for authority, whereas at other times an anti-authority complex results (Sutherland, 1929:44). For example, punishment of children (threats, beatings, or insults) may actually make them more likely to turn to crime in later years.

The increased complexity of modern society has created problems in understanding the relationship among conflict, law, and punishment. Conflict, Sutherland (1929) says, has been introduced into modern life principally as a result of greater geographic mobility and ease of communication. Alternative views and values find support in the heterogeneous environments that have developed in society, especially in urban areas. This development has led to increased interpersonal tensions in which disagreements in the application of the law are confounded by the interpretation of values and rights of different parties in the disputes. Also, regulating this conflict is made more difficult because the disputes are often outside the constraints provided by criminal law.

In the next few pages we will examine aspects of law and punishment as they have been reformulated in formal and informal approaches to the study of conflict. We can begin this discussion with Sutherland's sobering assessment that the reaction to conflict may be continued conflict, which tends to isolate the participants from each other without leading to any solution.

FORMAL AND INFORMAL LAW

Positivism versus Community Justice Approaches to Law

It has been argued that theories about the nature of law have failed to accommodate properly the tension that exists between legal and extralegal control in society. As Henry (1983) says, legal theorists view positive law as being independent of social processes. Positive law is an objective statement of rights and obligations that is administered according to a determination of the facts and adherence to due process. Social conditions or characteristics of disputants should not interfere with the determination of guilt or innocence in the pursuit of justice.

In response, community justice reformers decry the fact that law has become formal and bureaucratic. They argue that a more desirable legal ideal lies in an informalized, decentralized, popular or community form of justice. Law, they argue, has become separated from ordinary people, unaccountable, discretionary, and riddled with expensive delays and ineffective controls (Henry, 1983:38). These reformers have called for alternatives to the rigidity of the formal courts that administer positive law. Informal courts have appeared as forums in which complaints and grievances can be dealt with in terms that the grievants understand and in a climate of conciliation rather than of confrontation. These have included such areas as neighborhood mediation programs (discussed in some detail in Chapter 5).

Henry argues against this separation of informal and formal justice. To liberate people from the constraints of positive law, he states, an awareness is required that informal sanctions are an integral part of the totality of law and not alternatives to it. That is, if participation in the administration of law simply leads to the separation of those who administer from those

who receive, there will have been no transformation in the conception of the delivery of justice, merely a change in personnel. The informal structure has no meaning outside of its relationship to the formal, just as the formal is meaningless without referring to the informal. The two are parts of the same whole (Henry, 1983:46).

This view echoes the warning made by Max Weber that discrediting formal law in favor of informal processes would not result in better justice. Rather, the judiciary would simply be transformed into a bureaucratized organization administering economic (contractual) relationships (Ewing, 1987:510). This result occurs because the *rightness* of formal justice comes into question, to be replaced by a strictly mechanical application of formal rules.

Whether or not it can be argued that law can contain basic rights and privileges for all in a fair and equitable way, it is clear that law cannot function outside of social context. An integrated theory of law must combine social structure and human action. Using this perspective, we need to look at law through the processes that bring it into being. That is, we need to look into the ways in which people interact to construct and reconstruct the ways in which law functions. This analysis requires an examination of typical social interchanges to see how interaction acquires the character of legal reality. We must also consider how interaction is conceptually differentiated into the formal and the informal, offense and response: "...in short how the reality formed in such conception is both autonomously generated and simultaneously bound by the totality of wider social structure" (Henry, 1983:68).

Law and Custom in Social Context

Moore (1973) argues that law is only one of a number of factors that affect the decisions people make, the actions they take, and the relationships they have. Consequently, important aspects of the connection between law and social change emerge only if law is inspected in the context of ordinary social life. The "rules of the game" that govern the operation of social life include some laws and some other quite effective norms and practices. These rules operate in "semi-autonomous social fields," where custom and law interact to control and constrain social behavior. As Silbey and Sarat (1987) argue, we must study families, schools, workplaces, social movements, and professional associations to present a broad picture of the role of law in society. We would then understand law not as something removed from life, occasionally operating on or regulating and shaping social forms, but as something fused with and inseparable from all social activities.

Examples drawn from sports help illustrate the relationship that exists between formal law, as dictated by the sports leagues, and custom, as determined by the participants. It is clear that the sports leagues tolerate certain "illegal" customs. If this were not the case we would have long ago seen the complete elimination of fighting in sports through the imposition of lengthy bans from the game. A five-minute penalty for fighting in hockey serves more to cool off the participants than to punish the behavior, especially as both disputants are generally assessed the same penalty (although hockey has now added a two-minute penalty for instigating the fight).

One could say that the formal rules state that fighting is illegal. It is simply that they are not severe enough or strictly enough enforced, which would mean that the authorities and participants are unhappy with the rule breaking and want a greater level of enforcement. However, after a game containing a bench-clearing brawl in Boston, the mayor threatened to send in the police to arrest combatants in future fights. The threat was met with great complaint by the National Hockey League officials, who claimed that what happened in hockey arenas was none of the mayor's business. The league sees itself as self-regulating, relying on its own administration of justice and custom (as expressed by players and fans) in the definition of acceptable transgressions of their written laws.

One player explained these laws in an interview published after a particularly scrappy hockey game. Marty McSorley, an NHL "tough guy," playing for the Edmonton Oilers, settled a score with a New Jersey Devil player who had jumped him in a game six months previously. McSorley was given an instigator minor, a fighting major, and a game misconduct. However, he felt it had been necessary to start the fight (and win it). The timing was perfect as the game was almost over and the Oilers had a comfortable lead. McSorley described his misdeed as having the full support of his teammates.

> I don't like having to do things like that but he'd (the New Jersey Devil player) set the precedent how a player should handle things like that. You've got to stand up and fight for your hockey club. Everybody was behind me. (*Edmonton Journal*, 1988:C1)

Macaulay (1987) argues that most complex societies rest on legal pluralism. There is an official law, but there are complementary, overlapping, and conflicting private legal systems, as well.

> School, television and film, and spectator sports offer versions of law that differ from that found in law schools. They also offer alternative resources from which people fashion their own understanding of what is necessary, acceptable, and just. (Macaulay, 1987:211)

The Quantity of Law

Seeing law as complementing custom assumes, as well, that the *quantity* of law in society varies with other aspects of social life, including social stratification, morphology, culture, organization, and social control (Black, 1979). Black argues that the extent to which law is invoked, in all respects, can be explained by variations in social structure and by the relative social positions of the disputants (e.g., victim and offender), without reference to how individual action or motivation affects the behavior of the law (Gottfredson & Hindelang, 1979:4).

Gottfredson and Hindelang (1979) set out to test Black's (1979) theory of law by using data drawn from the U.S. National Crime Survey. They report on the effects of Black's five social constructs on the mobilization of law when the victim called the police to report a criminal occurrence. These constructs are social status, operationalized as income differences between victim and offender; morphology measured by community size; employment status and marital status of victim; culture, measured by education of the victim and of the victim's neighborhood; organization, represented by the number of victims and offenders in the criminal act; and social control, indicated by the place where the victimization took place.

Gottfredson and Hindelang conclude from their analysis that in all cases, the use of law does not vary with these social constructs but only as a consequence of the seriousness of the crime. The more serious the crime, the more likely the victim is to invoke formal law. Thus, they argue, the use of criminal law depends primarily on what happens between the victim and the offender. The amount of harm suffered is the principal determinant of the quantity of law that is invoked (Gottfredson & Hindelang, 1979:5).

Black responds that "crime" itself explains why people call the police (Black, 1979:19). He criticizes Gottfredson and Hindelang's conclusions that severity determines the quantity of law because, he says, the National Crime Survey relies on victimization data, in which people themselves are asked to define, in their own terms, what is criminal and what is not. What people consider to be crime, Black argues, varies with its location and direction in social space. People define as criminal acts what takes place between strangers, such as assault, whereas this act may not be seen in the same way if it were to occur between intimates. The Gottfredson and Hindelang study, therefore,

> shows only what the labels predict, not what predicts the labels. It shows only whether people called the police when they considered an incident worthy of police attention, not whether some incidents were more or less likely to be considered worthy of this attention in the first place. (Black, 1979:21)

Black (1979) argues that seriousness is a social construct that can change according to social circumstance and custom. Further, it is stating the obvious to say that more serious crimes are reported to the police because the very reporting of them itself makes them more serious. Following Black's logic, crime becomes problematic when the situational factors in the social environment require a response. This response need not include calling the police, as self-help may have equally severe consequences.

The debate between Black and Gottfredson and Hindelang highlights the problems encountered in reconciling the operation of formal and informal law in society. It is clear, from the survey results presented in Chapter 3, what happens to those cases in which the police are *not* called. Forms of informal justice appear, differentiated in their application depending on the social relationship, custom, or social structure of the environment in which the event took place. Individuals will invoke informal solutions when confronted with a situation they feel they can handle themselves.

PUNISHMENT AND DETERRENCE

Law and Punishment

What is wrong with the law, in the public's eyes, is not the law itself but its enforcement (Currie, 1985). Robert Moore (1985:48) reports that there is consensus among Canadians that the laws generally stand for what people want. In addition, people say they obey the law because they believe it to be right. However, many are critical of the way in which justice is being dispensed. A majority indicate that something needs to be done to improve the way the legal system operates and the laws it produces. The public believes, further, that the law favors the rich and the powerful and that it takes too long to get anything done through the legal process. This negative view of justice extends to a feeling that there is less respect for the law and that fewer people are law-abiding than five years ago.

The degree of legal response to conflict and crime raises this question: How effective is the law in reducing criminality? Effectiveness is an issue in discussions of deterrence and public attitudes toward inadequate sentencing procedures. As Brillon (1985) points out, there is a disparity between the severity of the punishment that citizens want and the sentencing of criminals who committed serious crimes (e.g., homicide, rape, armed robbery). It is in the handling of dangerous criminals that people feel there is insufficient deterrence administered by the formal court system. This concern is reflected in the recent proposal by the Canadian government to tighten up the parole system. Under the current system, inmates are eligible for parole after serving one-third of their sentences. The proposed changes would require that one-half of the sentence be served before the inmate's case for parole can be reviewed. The Canadian Solicitor-General argued that these changes were being made to ensure an increase in "public safety" (*Globe and Mail*, 1988:1).

This response to criminality raises a question about the effective ways of providing deterrence, in that the law prescribes formal punishment for deviance but, in addition, communities set up informal mechanisms for the deterrence of undesirable (both criminal and noncriminal) behavior.

Deterrence

Nettler (1984a:111) says that those who believe that punishment does not deter are not using common sense. There are differential effects that apply, however, depending on the degree and probability of punishment. Deterrence theory focuses on a psychological process whereby individuals are discouraged from committing criminal acts only if they perceive legal sanctions as certain, swift, and/or severe (Williams & Hawkins, 1986). For example, Sherman and Berk (1984) support the deterrent effects of mandatory arrests in domestic assault cases. They have evidence that swift imposition of a sanction of temporary incarceration diminishes repeat offenses through **specific deterrence**. The support for arrest in cases of serious family violence has come at a time when there is increased concern about the ineffectiveness of informal sanction by family, neighbors, and police who try to mediate solutions in these cases.

Perceptions that the law provides insufficient deterrence are reinforced by widespread stories of the breakdown of the justice system in punishing offenders. Examples are provided by two widely publicized cases in Massachusetts of vehicular homicide because of drunk driving. In the first case, the individual had been convicted nine times previously and was driving without a license. The media's treatment of this problem focused on the repeat offenses. There is a strong drunk driving law in Massachusetts, which the governor has emphasized in TV commercials. What is at fault, in the public's view, is a system that allows someone to get away with multiple offenses. Short of throwing him in jail for the rest of his life, however, how does one deter such an individual from repeating this crime?

In the other case, the vehicular homicide occurred while the driver was waiting for trial on a previous offense of drunk driving. When he was being tried for the second offense, his drunken friends showed up at the court to see him. Is the problem here that the courts are too lenient or that individuals are not afraid of the consequences of going to court or going to jail? Direct sanction by the courts must be complemented with indirect negative sanction among peers for being arrested and jailed for committing illegal acts.

If persons anticipate that others will disapprove of their arrest for committing a certain act, and they refrain from that activity because they fear the stigma of getting caught, this would be counted as an instance of **general deterrence**, with a legal sanction as the source (Williams & Hawkins, 1986). Alternatively, if the risk of arrest is seen as low and the severity of punishment minimal, individuals might still be prevented from committing a crime by the stigmatizing reactions of others. In this case, the fear of stigma stems from the act, not the sanction, and thus is extralegal (Williams & Hawkins, 1986:563).[1]

Extralegal factors, including concern about health, morality, and the social influence of peers, are more important in deterring use of marijuana than the fear of legal punishment (Meier & Johnson, 1977). Social morality may be internalized, on the one hand, or administered through example or coercion in primary relationships that exist in the community, on the other hand. Paternoster, and colleagues (1983) pursue this idea in their research on the influence of perceived risk versus informal social control on the likelihood of becoming involved in criminal action. They take panel data drawn from a sample of U.S. college students to determine the different effects that experience with previous criminal behavior versus perception of current risk of punishment have on actual behavior measured at a second period in time. In the analysis, the researchers control for the influence of social bonds, that is, commitments people have to certain self-defined goals; attachment they feel to others, especially family and friends; involvement they have in activities, including socializing with others; and beliefs they express about right or wrong.

The concern over the risk of getting caught (the deterrent effect) has little impact on whether or not criminal behavior is pursued when beliefs, attachments, commitment, and informal social influences are entered into the equation (Paternoster et al., 1983). One must also account for the extent of knowledge of sanctions (Henshel, 1978; Teevan, 1976). People are more concerned about what other people think about their getting caught than about the actual probability of getting caught. These findings fly in the face of the belief that only through strong penal sanction will individuals be deterred from criminal action.

Of course, it may be that deterrence has an indirect effect on personal, informal relationships. Potential offenders fear the criminal justice system because arrest might provoke the disrespect of family and peers (Tittle, 1980). Or as Williams and Hawkins (1986:559) state about the Paternoster research, it may be that the perceived certainty of legal sanctions simply strengthens one's belief that others condemn the act. As Currie says in reporting on research by Shannon, most young people that were studied in

---

[1] This is a case for deterrence by strong social bonds, as addressed in Chapter 2.

Racine, Wisconsin, had committed crime serious enough to merit arrest but most of them had stopped by age 18. Less than 8 percent said that they had quit because they were afraid of being caught and punished. Most reassessed their behavior in the context of the problems it caused with family, friends, or school and expressed concern about what this behavior would do in adversely affecting their future in the community (Currie, 1985:57).

We can argue in one of two ways concerning deterrence. Strong legal sanction may be necessary to reinforce the negative effects of arrest on relationships with others. Alternatively, we could argue that our fixation on formal response has led us to believe that the system needs to become more punitive in order to deter crime. It may be, in fact, that the system has simply usurped too much of the deterrence role and left the informal system without the ability to provide this sanction. Tittle (1980) makes the point that the severity of informal sanction has been ignored altogether in the deterrence research. The difference in perception of severity may be a difference in the perception of the loss of social bonds that occurs with the punishment being exacted. Consistent with the point made by Nettler (1984a) that punishment deters, this punishment need not be legal. It can be just as effective coming from a withdrawal of affection or the weakening of social bonds.

Self-Help, Avoidance, and Informal Deterrence

Deterrence must also be seen in the context of **crime as social control** (Black, 1983). Far from being an intentional violation of a prohibition, some crime is moralistic and involves the pursuit of justice.

> It is a mode of conflict management, possibly a form of punishment, even capital punishment. Viewed in relation to law, it is self-help. To the victim—as deviant, crime is social control. (Black, 1983:34)

In a related way, Black argues that victimizations may be deterred by self-help rather than—or in addition to—law (Black, 1983:39).

The concept of self-help brings together punishment and informal conflict management. The deterrence provided by knowledge of possible retribution is of a different kind than that supported by formal law. The use of crime to deter crime is more widespread and effective than is commonly accepted by criminologists, as it is not precluded by justice system capacity (Pontell, 1978). Further, the courts favor leniency in responding to crimes committed as self-help, in recognition of its strong deterrent effect. For example, there was the recent case of a Calgary pharmacist who gunned down in the street an armed robber who was fleeing from the scene of the crime. Although charged with second degree murder, the pharmacist was acquitted on the basis of self-defense.[2]

Affecting the belief in the viability of informal control strategies, including self-help, is the oft-repeated sentiment that North American society has witnessed a breakdown in community structures. This breakdown has led to the necessity for large-scale formal institutions to bring about the maintenance of order. The family and the schools have both failed to contain the disruptive forces of transiency and heterogeneity, which cause the breakdown of social ties and the restraining action of informal sanctions.

This view leads to the conclusion expressed by Geerken and Gove (1975) that since deterrence is linked to communication patterns, it should be most effective in small, simple societies, where the deterrence message can be clearly transmitted through a highly integrated set of interpersonal relations. But as Tittle (1980) points out, there is the counter argument that deterrence should operate most effectively where there are no other constraints on behavior and where the extralegal conditions conducive to crime are the greatest, that is, in large, heterogeneous, and unintegrated places (Zimring & Hawkins, 1973).

As an alternative to self-help, individuals may simply avoid dealing with conflict. Many disputes (including those that could be defined as criminal) may remain unresolved because the "victim" simply finds it easier not to continue. This avoidance may include "lumping it" or moving away—which raises some important issues related to the reduced role of deterrence in modern society.

The evidence seems to support the idea that the informal controls that exist in simple societies are also evident in the less integrated modern societies, although the ability to avoid sanction is obviously greater. Felstiner (1975) says that in North American society, avoidance is common, partly because of the lack of community solidarity needed to provide ongoing mediation of interpersonal disputes. North American society relies instead on adjudication and the concomitant deterrent effect of legal sanction. What avoidance can mean for deterrence is that without informal response, much crime will remain undeterred.

The evidence presented in Chapter 3 from victimization surveys indicates that a number of would-be complainants do not proceed through the regular police and court system. They do not want the offender to be harmed or they think that the incident is a private, not a criminal, matter (Merry, 1979). The possibility of ostracism, not the stigmatization of criminality, is used as deterrent. Effective deterrence involves community·con-

---

[2] Paradoxically, by definition of the court, he has not legally committed a crime at all.

trol, reducing the emphasis on punishment and increasing collective responsibility.

Informal community structures may, however, encourage individuals to deal with disputes instead of avoiding them. When they do, the fear of punishment from legal authorities may be diminished in importance. In other words, if avoidance is curtailed by community custom, the deterrence of law is reduced because informal justice (including crime as self-help) can deter instead. It is when avoidance is precluded by public or private justice systems that the deterrent effect of law should increase.

This discussion does not center on the rightness or wrongness of deterrence strategies but rather on the extent to which the elements for informal sanction are available in contemporary society. Juxtaposing formal with informal deterrence provides an important contrast in how we respond to crime. Focusing on the informal structures, in addition, need not address the inevitability of crime or disputes, only the ways in which they are to be eliminated.

INSTITUTIONAL RESPONSES TO CRIME AND CONFLICT

Correctional Strategies

McCarthy and McCarthy (1984) provide a useful categorization of **correctional** responses to crime. These account differentially for the role that conflict plays in contributing to crime. First, **restraint** operates to isolate the offender from other members of the community, restricting his or her freedom in taking part in "normal" day-to-day activities in society. In this case, neither changes in the offender nor community interests are highly valued. This perspective is gaining greater popularity in response to the public demands for retribution and punishment. Its consequence is more crowded jails.

Second, **reform** emphasizes compliance with community standards, and rewards and punishments are used to develop it. The expectations of the community are summarized as "learn a skill, get a job, and stay out of trouble" (McCarthy & McCarthy, 1984:7). Third, the **rehabilitation** model is based on the premise that offenders need individual treatment to gain maturity and responsibility; professional therapists have developed programs to change the thoughts and actions of inmates. This model has caused great controversy over the last two decades. It places the greatest emphasis on the individual, with little or no consideration of community expectations.

Finally, **reintegration** works from the belief that crime and delinquency are as much symptoms of community disorganization as they are evidence of behavioral problems of individuals. Community-based corrections programs emphasize the elements of reintegration as a way of using the informal mechanisms of the community (the development of social bonds) to constrain the individual and reduce the likelihood of recidivism.

Rehabilitation versus Restraint

The rehabilitation model promotes the idea of treatment in institutions. It is intended to create "new" individuals who can fit into society in a constructive and positive way. Silberman (1976) says there is support for the hypothesis that those who associate with others who are criminally involved are likely themselves to become involved. The introduction of moral tones to the negative labeling of acts will deter illegal behavior, not the threat of punishment. It is on this basis that moral rehabilitation becomes the prescription for deterring crime by potential offenders.

Determinism and **correctionalism** characterize the rehabilitative ideal.

> Determinism, by denying responsibility for criminal behavior and hence individual rationality, allegedly eroded the dignity of offenders and made them passive objects of social policy; correctionalism, under the guise of benevolence, supposedly encouraged disparate treatment of offenders and permitted an unjustifiable degree of state intervention into their lives. (Cavender, 1984:204)

Complaints about this approach to rehabilitation have focused on treatment that acts as a form of punishment, especially where individuals were being subjected to these programs against their will. As reported by Martin, Sechrest, and Redner (1981), coerced therapy to correct offenders is seen by some as degrading, unsuccessful, and potentially repressive.

Further, despite its grounding in normative structure of society, the rehabilitative model has run into some serious difficulties in recent years partly because of its lack of success in promoting crime prevention. The rehabilitative ideal is condemned as an ineffective crime control strategy when evaluated in terms of recidivism, that is, the tendency for individuals to reoffend (Cavender, 1984). It is seen, in addition, as a policy that fosters unfairness. For example, there is strong disagreement concerning its use in treating individuals. The bias of middle-class agencies trying to create middle-class values in offenders is seen as an insensitive and unrealistic objective. Nettler (1984b) argues that rehabilitation promotes the fabrication that we are reconstructing something that did not exist in the first place.

Experiences with rehabilitation lead to a position that "nothing works" (Martinson, 1974). Rehabilitation programs, it is argued by some, encourage crime through a lack of deterrence. The feeling among those who criticize the rehabilitation model is that it is soft on crime, providing excuses for individuals to continue to be involved in deviant behavior, especially as they perceive that there will be no penalty attached to this action. These arguments promote the restraint model, which emphasizes improving the organizational structure of prisons to provide isolation and punishment to offenders in direct proportion to the seriousness of their crimes.

Wilson and Herrnstein argue that rehabilitation is a liberal ideal set against retribution. It represents a belief that the offender is *driven* to his or her crimes, rather than committing them freely and intentionally (Wilson & Herrnstein, 1985:505). An act deserves punishment, according to the principle of equity, if it is committed in the absence of certain explicit circumstances. One of these circumstances is insanity, but they can also include duress, provocation, entrapment, mistake, and accident. Society directs its disapproval, when it punishes, at the sources of the behavior that it must constrain: malice, lust, treachery, greed, envy, cruelty, hatred, and other precipitating impulses toward crime.

> By proving that excusing conditions are absent and then punishing, the criminal justice system sharply outlines for its citizens the choice between crime and non-crime and then makes sure that the appropriate conditions are attached to each alternative. To the extent that excusing conditions can be demonstrated, punishment should be mitigated or totally suspended. (Wilson & Herrnstein, 1985:506)

This view leaves open the question of whether or not the elements of conflict in society that may promote the movement toward crime can be considered extenuating circumstances. Currie (1985) has argued that the inability or unwillingness to deal with family violence has led to a situation in which we tolerate interpersonal violence that would be unacceptable between strangers. The extenuating circumstances in this case involve the preservation of family relations. Yet the conditions continue to demand punishment.

This example is only one demonstration that there are no cut and dried boundaries for punishment alluded to by Wilson and Herrnstein, any more than there are defined outlines of what is criminal and what is not. In addition, there is a need to consider the degree to which the individuals being punished feel that the sentence is fair, is punitive, and reflects a threat to their continuation of the criminal behavior after their release from jail.

Currie (1985:236) argues that it is one thing to criticize the oppressive or trivial character of so much of what has passed for treatment of criminals but quite another to reject the idea of rehabilitation altogether. Rejecting the idea, he says, requires us to believe that offenders do not have problems big enough to need help in overcoming them or that society has no responsibility for seeing that they get help if they need it. He believes that the "nothing works" mentality is not supported when careful programs have been devised to deal with offenders and there has been consistent follow-up in community support.

Martin, Sechrest, and Redner (1981) repeat this sentiment in their call for wider sentencing options and more effective institutional and community rehabilitation programs. This point is particularly of interest to us here, both in our understanding of how we are to respond to the conflict bases of crime and in our understanding of the role that the community plays in providing ongoing support for programs that alleviate these problems.

Currie (1985) talks about reducing the conditions that are conducive to crime through the actions of the police, through structural changes in the economy, and through the involvement of the community in crime prevention. He sees that there has been an inadequate conceptualization of the community, especially among liberal criminologists. Further, crime prevention has been couched in individual terms, when a large part of the problem in the enhancement of crime is the weakening of communal institutions that are the bedrock of social order.

> Much of the liberal emphasis on rehabilitation, for instance, meant "individual treatment" without regard for the familial or communal networks from which the offenders came and to which they would return; much crime "prevention" involved the provision of services to deprived individuals, less often measures to strengthen the resources of their families and neighborhoods. (Currie, 1985:228)

Because of the apparent problems in rehabilitation, however, the conservative approach has developed much appeal. At the same time, there is some feeling among conservatives that, at least in terms of crime prevention, there is room for the community to act. This attitude seems motivated by the desire to decarcerate, thereby saving government resources in paying for institutions and activating volunteers to take responsibility for community programs. The desire to switch to volunteer action is offered as a way of taking the cost out of community services, a view seen as unrealistic given the need for money from grants to support these programs (see Currie, 1985:262).

Reintegration

Ducker says that the rehabilitation model, which has been seen with increased disdain in many circles, needs to be replaced by a "justice" model. He reports that studies of violence in prisons have found that inmates' certainty of early parole and their ability to predict and modify the length of their sentence can reduce prison violence. Even more important, "cultivation of a sense of fair dealing in prisoners can be influential in their rehabilitation" (Ducker, 1983–84:150). By this, we assume that prisoners are less likely to be recidivists if they acquire a sense of rules and fair play.

This is a powerful concept to follow. It addresses the need for prevention rather than reaction in dealing with criminality. Elements of this approach are drawn from social control theory, which emphasizes the role that strong ties can play in bringing a sense of justice and fair play into social relations. Where this sense is missing, the call by third parties to disputants to use rules of order in resolving conflicts must become louder. An experiment in bringing this management to the community is contained in what has been referred to as **community corrections**. As with rehabilitation, this approach has many critics. It has importance for our discussion, however, in light of the attention we have paid to community conflict as a source of crime.

Not all approaches to the community rely on the resources of neighbors, families, or friends to sustain them. In fact, there has been a strong movement in the direction of community-based corrections that requires the allocation of large-scale professional action in the community to provide alternatives to institutions. McCarthy and McCarthy (1984) define *community-based corrections* as the general term used to refer to various types of therapeutic, support, and supervision programs for criminal offenders. These include diversion, pretrial release, probation, restitution and community service, halfway houses, and parole. All these programs, they claim, attempt to maintain the offender's existing ties to the community and to establish new ones.

Included in the list of options available for pretrial diversion are mediation programs, which are seen as providing alternatives to the courts for individuals involved in disputes. Probation, an often-used method of community-based corrections, is exercised at the discretion of the judge on the condition that there is no repeat offense and the terms of the probation (including, at times, counseling and supervision by probation officers) are met.

There is an assumption implicit in this approach that the prison system will not appreciably add to the individual's punishment and that the community is not well served in paying for this individual's incarceration. A similar motive supports parole. This is an area that has received much greater public attention because of the fear of dangerous offenders with parole-shortened sentences appearing on the street. The current debate over parole in Canada has focused attention on the public's negative attitude toward the release of inmates back into the community after serving only a part of their sentence. The call for more punitiveness has elicited the response from one politician that abandoning parole only delays the inevitable release of the offender. The problem is less a concern over incarceration, then, and more a question of how the public will receive these individuals back into their midst.

Despite the enthusiasm of supporters of community-based corrections, such as McCarthy and McCarthy (1984), the community that individuals are to be integrated back into often does not exist. Scull (1984:161) recounts the difficulties involved in getting residents of urban areas to take placement of ex-inmates of any kind in their neighborhood. In addition, families have difficulty providing the sustained social support that is needed to individuals who come out of institutions. As a result, individuals are managed by formal rather than informal institutions, which has led to a widening of the network of social control (Scull, 1984). Diversion programs are simply extensions of institutional control over offenders. Diversion takes on a character of referral from one part of the system to another. It is not clear, then, that we have reintegration as much as restraint without walls. The idea of community corrections based on a preventive rather than reactive model makes a great deal of sense, despite the practical problems that have developed in reducing this conflict. It requires, however, a commitment by the community to get involved in the process of conflict resolution, a topic of the next chapter.

SUMMARY

Legal theorists have viewed positive law as being independent of social processes. This perspective ignores the role that the community can play in providing an informal, decentralized, and popular form of justice. Law must combine social structure with human action. The quantity of law, then, becomes reflective of societal custom and the organizational structure of agencies of social control.

This connection of law to society is demonstrated in the role that law plays in deterring crime and dictating punishment. Formal law must be seen as being complemented by informal justice in raising deterrence and inflicting punishment. The latter can be seen in the context of self-help and its alternative, avoidance. If avoidance increases, formal law provides a deterrent to misbehavior that may lead to crime. However, if community solidarity is high with low levels of avoidance, less law is needed as a deterrent. Informal control should impose sanctions on this misbehavior. Accompanying lower levels of avoidance, though, is self-help. With increases in self-help there is less of a need for law. At the same time, there may be a need to deter self-help that is itself crime-based.

The role of law focuses on the prescribed responses we make to conflict. These responses can be interpreted differently through mediation, police programs, and the courts. We can begin the investigation of these responses by reviewing the efforts that have been made to manage community conflict through alternative dispute resolution.

CHAPTER 5

Mediation, Disputes, and Crime

INTRODUCTION

In an effort to pose alternative structures to mediate and resolve interpersonal disputes that emerge in contemporary society, the Alternative Dispute Resolution (ADR) movement has developed. As Adler argues, the ADR movement has been fueled by the social legitimation of the bargaining process itself. "What has been discovered, or perhaps rediscovered, is that many disputes that are traditionally conceptualized and treated as collisions of rights or win-lose adversarial contests, are indeed negotiable" (Adler, 1987:61). The practical roots of this perspective derive from the debate that has emerged in the legal profession concerning the appropriateness of alternative (or informal) justice systems residing alongside the more conventional ones. The systemic problems of court capacity and the orientation toward more responsive (or natural) law has led to a debate over the suitability of options for conflict resolution (Harrington, 1985).

Further, the question of the ability of North American society to accommodate the opportunities that alternative dispute strategies offer has brought out a number of both supportive and negative views. As a positive force, these strategies may bring justice back to the community (Danzig and Lowy, 1975). As a negative force, they may impose unequal justice on individuals who cannot afford formal justice procedures (Abel, 1982). In this chapter, we will examine the recent experience with mediation as an alternative to the imposition of formal justice solutions to community conflict, including criminal action. Important in this discussion is the paradoxical finding that although alternative dispute resolution is promoted widely as a better way than the courts of dealing with most conflict, it is rarely used by disputants. It has, however, raised some important issues for the ways in which police and the courts have begun to address community concerns about the administration of justice.

STRATEGIES OF CONFLICT RESOLUTION

Dispute Resolution

Figure 5.1 outlines a spectrum of available processes for resolving disputes (Sander, 1982). On the extreme left of the diagram is **adjudication**. This is a decision-making process in which a third party is presented with proofs and arguments for a decision in each disputant's favor. A fact-finding **inquiry** resembles a typical adjudication, but the inquiry officer normally has no coercive power and, often, there is no agreed-on form of presentation and participation of interested parties. In **mediation** and **conciliation** the two disputants are brought together with a third person, who hears their case, makes suggestions for resolution, but leaves it to the disputants to come to their own resolution. **Negotiation** requires that the two parties attempt to work out their own solution without the assistance of a third party. **Avoidance** means that no attempt to negotiate takes place. Of greatest interest to us here is the contrast between adjudication, as practiced by the courts through formal law, and mediation, which has its roots in informal justice.

The Mediation Process

According to Cooley (1986), mediation is a process in which an impartial intervenor helps disputants reach a voluntary settlement of their differ-

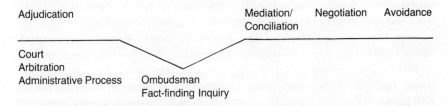

Figure 5.1. Spectrum of Dispute Resolution Strategies (Source: Frank Sander, "Varieties of Dispute Processing." In Roman Tomasic and Malcolm Feeley [eds.], *Neighborhood Justice: An Assessment of an Emerging Idea*, White Plains, N.Y.: Longman Inc., 1982, pp. 25–43.)

ences through an agreement that defines future behavior. This process involves eight stages: initiation, preparation, introduction, problem statement, problem clarification, generation and evaluation of alternatives, selection of alternatives, and agreement. To start, the mediation process may be initiated in two ways. Parties may submit a request directly to the mediation organization, or the dispute may be referred to mediation by court order or rule in a court-annexed mediation program. In the preparation of the case, the mediator is informed about the parties and features of the dispute, including aspects of the disputants' relationship and factors that will assist or inhibit resolution.

In the introductory phase of the mediation process, most often the first joint session, the mediator establishes his or her acceptability, integrity, credibility, and neutrality (Cooley, 1986:266). The mediator must meet certain objectives at the outset. These include, according to Cooley, establishing control of the process, determining issues and positions of the parties, getting the agreement-forging process started, and encouraging the continuation of direct negotiations.

At the problem definition stage, there are two possible ways of laying out the areas of disagreement. First, both parties can give their positions and discuss each issue as it is raised, or all the disagreements first can be briefly identified, with more detailed exploration of these areas of contention left to a later time. When the problem is laid out, the mediator helps clarify the issues, bringing out the important points of disagreement between the two parties. This clarification can take place in separate discussions with each party. In a subsequent joint session these disagreements are summarized by the mediator for both parties to agree on (Cooley, 1986:267).

Once the issues have been defined, the mediator will try to bring the parties together. In generating and evaluating alternatives, the mediator tries to get individuals to soften their positions and to see different ways of defining their problems, thereby offering new ways to solve them. The alternatives that emerge are suggested by the disputants, and the mediator guides the selection of the best of these alternative agreements. A final settlement produces the optimum results with which both parties can live.

Before the termination of the mediation process, the mediator summarizes the new positions and clarifies the terms of the agreement that has been achieved, securing the assent of both parties (sometimes by signing a written form). This, then, is a product of the negotiation between the disputants and is not imposed on them by a third party.[1]

In mediation, when norms collide, account is taken of both sets

---

[1] For a detailed account of mediation as practiced in a community setting, see Beer (1986).

of values (Eisenberg, 1976:644). Also, an assessment must be made of whether or not it is important to reduce the tension that builds up in a conflict. It has to be determined whether on not there is a need to find a winner, a decision that may be influenced by a desire to uphold the principles of fair play and equity. All these factors may play a small role in adjudicated settlements (Eisenberg, 1976).

Mediation as an Alternative to Courts

Mediation has been offered as an alternative to the courts in resolving the ongoing conflicts that occur in urban neighborhoods, as described in Chapter 3, especially those between people who have continuing relationships in which avoidance is difficult (e.g., relatives and neighbors). These disputes are hard to resolve in the courts. Judges find it difficult to treat more than the symptoms of conflict (Stulberg, 1975:361).

> Much like the visible tip of an iceberg, the private criminal complaint frequently deals with relatively minor charges growing out of deeper human conflict, frustration, and alienation; the criminal law with its focus on the defendant alone is ill equipped to deal with this basic fact. A judge faced with a crowded court calendar, "beyond reasonable doubt" criterion for conviction and conflicting stories, will often dismiss these "minor offences" and admonish the defendant not to engage in similar conduct in the future, perhaps threatening possible punishment for future offenses. This is not conflict resolution; it is not problem solving in the community, nor is it intended to be. (Stulberg, 1975:361)

Following this line of argument, Danzig proposes that the police cannot keep the streets safe from crime, the courts are unable to establish guilt or innocence of individuals brought to trial, and the prison system inspires recidivism as frequently as it reduces it. In sum, he says, there is a strong case that America's criminal justice system neither controls nor corrects criminality (Danzig, 1982:2).

Stulberg[2] maintains, further, that the tendency for our society to over-criminalize human conduct creates several risks. The courts may be inundated with cases, thereby imposing undesirable time pressures on judges to deal adequately with their case load. Further, the constraints imposed by the rules of evidence and the requirements of due process may lead to dismissal of specific charges even though it is clear that the dispute remains unresolved between the parties involved. In addition, the courts may find a party guilty but lack the resources to provide an adequate

---

[2] Following Morris and Hawkins (1969).

remedy for the situation, leading to a meaningless judgment and ineffective justice (Stulberg, 1975:360), a point made in Chapter 1 (Hagan, 1985).

Danzig (1982) proposes that this poor fit between criminality and institutions can be resolved through the implementation of a decentralized or "neighborhood-based" system of criminal justice. This system is attractive for three reasons. First, decentralization may improve the operation of the police, the courts, and the prisons by bringing home the responsibilities of these institutions to the community, and vice versa. The direct relationship that is established between these institutions and the community provides greater sympathy and understanding, as well as greater involvement in day-to-day operations of the community. This interdependence among police, courts, and community has taken on some of these characteristics in the movement toward community policing that has become popular in recent years. This approach will be discussed in greater detail in our review of the police in the next chapter.

The second reason for decentralization, according to Danzig (1982), is the advantage of providing physical proximity of the courts and jails to the community in which the offender lives. This proximity allows for the maintenance of social ties with the offender, an important aspect of using the community as a control agent over future actions of the deviant individual.[3]

Third, the decentralization of institutions allows for the use of para-professionals, who are more in tune with the concerns of the community than are the legal professionals who operate in the courts. This use of local volunteers is an essential element in most community-based mediation. The structuring of community resources in this way provides an environment into which offenders can be released, as well as creating restraints to offending in the first place.

Danzig does not argue for the dismantling of the centralized court system but rather proposes a complementary system be created to handle local concerns on a customized basis. He suggests a community court to handle such issues as family disputes, some marital issues, juvenile delinquency, landlord-tenant relations, breaches of contract, and minor misdemeanors. According to Danzig, the professional family court treats parties only in the courtroom. We must recognize that people's problems are resolved or intensified, if not caused, by the milieu in which they dwell (Danzig, 1982:16). This view is consistent with that argued previously: that many crimes develop as a result of the escalation of disputes from the social environment of the disputants. The idea of a community court has had

---

[3] This factor is closely related to a community corrections perspective.

many supporters and, in fact, has led to a variety of experiments with community mediation programs throughout North America.

Our interest in mediation programs arises from the fact that they are an attempt to provide an organized response to conflict in the community. Further, they are a way of dealing informally with disputes that may become more serious should they be left untreated or allowed to escalate to the point where they can be dealt with only through the police and courts in their most extreme form.

In practice, mediation has been quite selective in the problems it has attracted. Snyder (1978) reports that in the Dorchester, Massachusetts, program of mediation, the majority of cases involved people who were related or who knew one another and lived in close proximity to one another. As pointed out in Chapter 3, however, these types of disputes often ultimately end up in court. Conflicts involving threats and assaults are not as common between intimates as they are between strangers, which are often responded to with reciprocal violence.

In the Dorchester experiment, the referral agencies saw the most appropriate cases for mediation as those involving disputes with great hostility and, often, violent behavior (Snyder, 1978:764). Based on our findings as reported in Chapter 3, we would argue that greater attention should be directed at those less intimate relationships, which tend toward escalating conflict. The experience with mediation as reported by Snyder has had limited success in dealing with these types of problems.

As with cases brought to court, precedent plays an important role in the resolution of any dispute. In some cases, the past actions of individuals give the impression that a certain course of behavior has become a code of conduct. This view transforms precedents into principles of action, which are influential in the outcome of disputes. Sometimes, precedent will overcome logic and the merits of the case (Eisenberg, 1976:651). This form of conciliation may lead to frustration and escalation of further disputes in search of fairer solutions.

Further, mediators cannot ignore the facts of the dispute. Eisenberg (1976) maintains that in dispute negotiation, factual issues can be determined by explicit or tacit agreement between parties since the participants in the process have personal knowledge of most of the material facts. Where this personal knowledge does not exist, they can often agree on the truth of a proposition that affects the settlement. Eisenberg feels that the insertion of a stranger as a third-party arbitrator (such as a judge) into the situation changes this agreement on facts. There is often a need for a reconstruction of the basic issues of the case. This need for a redefinition of the terms of the dispute causes problems for swift determination of these facts and the decision about solutions.

The transformation of the conflict to terms that make sense to the arbitrator reflects the complaint voiced by Christie (1977) that the conflicts are stolen from the disputants and are changed to reflect the needs of the adjudication and not necessarily those of the people in conflict. However, the determination of the facts of the case may require such a transformation. This problem of fact finding has caused some severe difficulties in the appraisal of mediation efforts, especially when they involve the possibility of criminal sanction (Snyder, 1978). Reliance on the disputants themselves to lay out the facts of the case leaves the process open to corruption and unfairness.

In terms of the quality of the services offered, it appears that there is great satisfaction with the mediation process, although many cases that come through referral seem to fail. These results are confounded by the problems of accounting for the large number of cases that go back to the courts and fail to reach a solution there as well. The stability of agreed-on resolutions after mediation appears to be high. Merry (1982a) states, though, that there is really no absolute standard that we can use to establish a desirable or acceptable rate of stability. Further, a Vera Institute study (quoted in Tomasic, 1982:241) has questioned whether mediated settlements really are less likely to be broken than those settled through the courts.

An important incentive for mediation programs is the belief that they provide cheaper and more accessible conflict resolution than that afforded by the courts.[4] However, mediation is expensive, and it seems to be having little impact on case loads in the courts (Roehl & Cook, 1985:167). These costs are often a function of the long time involved in deliberating a dispute and in the new professionalism that is developing (taking these cases away from volunteers). The high costs may also be a function of the fact that the mediation programs are still new and small. The economies of scale may lessen the expense, but with the intensive nature of the process, this is not likely to have an appreciable effect.

Notwithstanding these problems, according to Roehl and Cook (1985) mediation is effective for those who try it, and for many disputes it is an extremely attractive and desirable alternative to court processing. It seems also to be true that mediation appears to work well because of the self-selection bias of those who volunteer for it. Mediation meets their incoming expectations by giving them what they are looking for, a forum that facilitates compromise and helps keep a relationship together.

---

[4] We will discuss issues related to access to court in Chapter 7.

NEIGHBORHOOD MEDIATION PROGRAMS

Community-based Mediation Centers

Tomasic (1982) sketches a history of the development of Neighborhood Justice Centers (NJC), which can be seen as important precursors of contemporary mediation programs. These programs, originally the conception of Danzig (1982), were refined and later recommended by the National Conference on the Causes of Popular Dissatisfaction with the Administration of Justice (the Pound Conference). Initial sites were funded by the federal government to serve as models throughout the United States.

Other programs in community mediation have also been developed. Stulberg reports on the creation of the National Center for Dispute Settlement, a division of the American Arbitration Association, "to search for a better way than the traditional prosecutorial approach to handle private criminal complaints of a misdemeanor nature" (Stulberg, 1975:360). This program was set up to take advantage of referrals from courts in which complainants are offered the choice of arbitration or court adjudication. In another application, the Night Prosecutor's Program, developed in Columbus, Ohio, was established to allow hearings in the evening so that antagonistic parties could resolve their disputes face to face as soon as possible after a criminal complaint had been filed (Palmer, 1975a, 1975b).

The goals of these programs include increasing speed in dispensing justice in minor criminal complaints, reducing court backlog, easing community and interpersonal relations, providing a forum for the working poor at times that does not conflict with their work, and removing the stigma of arrest records arising out of minor personal disputes (Palmer, 1975a:23). Similar programs include Neighborhood Small Claims Court in San Jose, California (Beresford & Cooper, 1977), and the Citizen Dispute Settlement Program in Dade County, Florida (Salas & Schneider, 1979).

In San Francisco there is a program providing community dispute services through the American Arbitration Association. It was set up to handle minor criminal disputes occurring between individuals with an ongoing relationship: landlords and tenants, employers and employees, domestic partners, and neighbors. Through the use of trained volunteers, this service seeks to bring the disputing parties together to negotiate a settlement that is mutually satisfactory. If, however, the disputants fail to reach an accommodation, the service provides for the arbitrator to make a legally binding award (American Arbitration Association, 1982).

Also in San Francisco, the Community Boards operate a community-based mediation program focusing on neighborhood, marital, and tenant-landlord conflicts. They report a case load of about 400 disputes a year, most of which come through self-referral. Half are resolved through conciliation. In Canada, the Kitchener-Waterloo Dispute Resolution Program has developed a referral process from prosecutors and police, with greatest emphasis on neighbor and friend conflicts. They claim a success rate of 25 percent of the 125 cases that they deal with annually. Clearly the numbers of cases that come to these groups are small, and the success rates are not as high as those reported by individuals who set out to solve these problems themselves, as reported in Chapter 3.

New York State has developed a Community Dispute Resolution Centers Program. The state government passed a law in 1985 making these centers a permanent part of the Unified Court System (Christian, 1985). This law (Chapter 91, Laws of 1985) allows the centers to make monetary awards upon consent of the parties that are not to exceed the monetary jurisdiction of the small claims part of the justice court ($1,500). Between its inception in 1981 and 1985, the 46 centers in place have had 224,000 contacts and referrals. There were 56,000 conciliations, mediations, and arbitrations. Of these, 77 percent of the referrals came from the courts, 6 percent from the police and sheriffs' departments, and 5 percent from district attorneys. Another 6 percent walk into the centers, bypassing the traditional justice system. These centers handle more than just civil disputes. Included in their mandate are criminal disputes as well as domestic and harassment matters and assaults.

There are also some programs that direct special attention to the conflicts that emerge between adults and children. An example is the Forum, developed as part of the Neighborhood Youth Diversion Program in the Bronx, New York, to deal with problems that would most often find their way into juvenile court (Statsky, 1974). Mediation in schools is also offered as a way of promoting conflict resolution among children (American Bar Association, 1985). Programs for "persons in need of supervision" (PINS) have also been developed to handle cases in which children are out of parental control (Roehl & Cook, 1985).

The Canadian experience with mediation programs has not been as extensive as that in the United States. As Horrocks (1982) points out, the government has shown little interest in funding such endeavors, except in the area of family mediation. Most of the support for the programs that do exist comes from private foundations or from law foundations (although the Kitchener-Waterloo program reports getting some federal government funding). The lack of interest in Canada in alternative justice may derive from differences in the administration of the law and the disinclination of police and community agencies to refer matters to volunteer groups for resolution.

In a review of agencies listed in the Dispute Resolution Program Directory compiled by the Special Committee on Alternative Dispute Resolution of the American Bar Association (ABA) (American Bar

Association, 1986), there were 304 programs designated in 1986–87, not all of which were active. By the calculation reported by the ABA, a quarter of these programs were established within the previous four years. The majority of their funding came from local or state governments. Some rely on private sources. This statistic seems to indicate the reduced influence of "community models," which evolved from the belief that unlike the agency models, with their close ties to the courts, they should be operated at the grass roots with independent funding.

Further evidence of the growth of agency-based programs is the indication that a small minority rely on walk-in or word-of-mouth referral. The majority of the cases come to them through court, police, and community agency referrals (Pipkin & Rifkin, 1984:210). In addition, Pipkin and Rifkin report a strong move toward the professionalization of program staff, moving it away from the volunteer base that was considered an important element in the development of successful conciliation.

The Multi-Door Courthouse

A new program to integrate mediation and other alternative dispute resolution programs into the court system is referred to as the "multi-door courthouse." Sponsored by the American Bar Association's Special Committee on Dispute Resolution, Multi-Door Courthouse projects were started in 1984 in the District of Columbia, Houston, and Tulsa. According to Finkelstein (1986), the Multi-Door Courthouse utilizes a sophisticated screening and referral option that is both visible and accessible to the public. Through a central Intake Center, people are educated about the alternatives available to them in resolving their disputes. The basic tool for the Washington, D.C., staff is a comprehensive referral manual, which includes descriptions of over 300 dispute resolution, legal, and social service programs in the community.

> With general information about dispute resolution techniques and specific information about basic services, eligibility standards, and operational procedures of individual programs, Intake Specialists familiarize disputants with their options, suggest the best approach for the resolution of particular disputes, and recommend specific programs which are potentially of greatest use. (Finkelstein, 1986:305)

The Multi-Door program is also initiating experiments of its own, including a mediation program for minor criminal, delinquency, and PINS cases. Contact is made with prosecutors to gain agreement to ensure routine diversion from the criminal justice system into mediation. In appropriate cases, an enforceable restitution contract is worked out between the parties through a mediation procedure (Finkelstein, 1986:136).

Conflict Management in Prisons

Dinitz argues for the extension of mediation programs into prisons. The growth of interpersonal violence there seems connected to rapid internal changes in prison structure and organization and to the intrusion of conflicts from beyond the walls. By Dinitz's reckoning, since 1951 there has been a major prison riot in the United States every year. These riots have led to a greater public belief that punishment and therapy don't mix. The only reality, the public concludes, is the pain of punishment (Dinitz, 1983:158). Yet it appears that the rioting that took place in 1971 at Attica began almost spontaneously over a minor incident. The underlying issues of overcrowding, idleness, and inmate-guard hostility had been smoldering beneath the surface. It took only a small spark to ignite this mixture (Ducker, 1983–84:144).

Ducker says that the increase in rioting and the accompanying increase in judicial involvement in prisons, through civil action, has created a demand for alternative structures within the institutions to create a new balance in relations between prisoners and their keepers. The choice that seems to have gained popularity responds to the need for what Dinitz has called a "lawful prison." The informal order that has developed through the application of summary justice by correctional officers and the exploitation of inmate hierarchies to guarantee order needs to be replaced with institutionalized dispute resolution mechanisms to channel inmates' dissatisfaction and to create a sense of impartiality of treatment (Cole & Silbert, 1984; Ducker, 1983–84:149).

These objectives may be impossible to achieve in prison, however, based on research on inmate grievance procedures reported by Bordt and Musheno. They state that inmates in correctional institutions lack equality when entering into negotiations with prison officials over basic conditions, even when this negotiation is mandated as a preferred way of resolving problems. Bordt and Musheno conclude from their study that prison officials have the power to subvert legal settlements calling for revisions in correctional practices when no effective outside monitoring is secured as part of the implementation process. "Also, it shows how the implementation process, when dominated by bureaucratic interests, can transform a procedure intended to resolve disputes into a means of increasing social control as an effect" (Bordt & Musheno, 1988:22). This caution about the misuse of "mediation" in prisons has been repeated in its application in other areas. We can examine the criticisms of the mediation process, weighing the strengths of the arguments put forward by its supporters and detractors.

CRITICISMS OF THE MEDIATION PROCESS

Improper Applications of Mediation Principles

Merry (1982a) argues that, despite the good intentions of the individuals and institutions involved in providing mediation in the various programs offered throughout North America, these efforts could become a disappointing failure. The demise of these programs will occur, Merry argues, because of two factors. First, the underlying processes and social organization of mediation have been insufficiently understood. Second, the idea of mediation has been instituted in ways that are very different from what was foreseen by its original proponents. The centers that are being constituted to handle neighborhood justice differ from the prototypes. As a result, the mediation programs are failing to meet the needs of the community they were formed to serve because they are being asked to serve too many conflicting and contradictory interests (Merry, 1982a:173). The failures of mediation often reflect a poor understanding of disputes, as outlined in Chapter 3.

Merry (1982a) points out that the direct applicability to North American society of the models of mediation drawn from other societies— such as the community court described by Danzig (1982), which was modeled after the village moots in Liberia—is idealistic. These models promote the idea of conciliation, ignoring at the same time the important role of power, custom, and coercion in managing conflict. Mediators in other countries where this form of conflict resolution is practiced tend to be powerful and influential political leaders who enhance their position through their role of mediating conflict.

> Agreements focus on property and the payment of damages rather than the restoration of harmonious relationships and the promises of good behavior. Mediators are neither strangers nor indifferent, and are neutral only insofar as they have competing loyalties to both sides. A mediator is preeminently a representative of the moral code of his or her society and is never thought to function without reference to the dominant value system or previous decisions in similar cases. Further, the process of settling cases itself plays a crucial role in redefining and enunciating the rules of the society. (Merry, 1982a:173–174)

The transposition of the role of mediator as played out in small, homogeneous communities in village and pastoral societies to the inner-city neighborhoods of North America creates serious difficulties. The need for common experience, general agreement over similar standards of action and punishment, and acceptance of someone from within the community to provide informal mediation often transcends what is possible in transient, highly heterogeneous communities.

Mediation programs have been touted as providing the opportunity to turn away from the strangers individuals encounter in court settings and rely instead on people drawn from their own communities. Tomasic (1982:224) questions this assumption of familiarity, pointing out that many mediators are drawn from court bureaucracy, such as the probation service. The professionalization of the mediation process (Pipkin & Rifkin, 1984) clearly draws on mediators even further from the community. Volunteer mediators are still used, according to Pipkin and Rifkin, in public agencies, where their lower level of expertise attracts disputes of less complexity.

The Demand for Justice

The demand for "justice," which people see as universal standards of the application of the law, is not amenable to the less fixed standards followed in the conciliation process (Merry, 1982b). Individual disputants must first agree on the process to be followed and accept the mediating role of the intermediary. This is a problem that is not found in societies in which this mediation process has been accepted as a normal part of community function, however.

Coupled with this view of mediation as having loose standards is the view that it offers second-class justice (Goldberg, Green, & Sander, 1986; Hensler, 1986). The point has been made that alternatives will shunt low- and middle-income disputants to a justice system consisting primarily of semicoerced compromise settlements, whereas the so-called first-class justice offered by the courts will be available only to the rich and powerful. In responding to this view, Goldberg and colleagues pose the question, "What is first class justice?"

> If it is defined as a method of resolving disputes that includes legal representation, formal rules of procedure, and resolution based upon law, then those alternatives that are mediatory in nature will inevitably be labelled second class, and the central question essentially answers itself. If, however, first class justice is defined as that dispute resolution process which most satisfies the participants...research has been done, and uniformly concludes that participants in the alternative processes are as satisfied or more satisfied with those processes than are participants in court adjudication. (Goldberg, Green, & Sander, 1986:295–296)

Research findings provided by Hensler (1986) on court-annexed arbitration in civil disputes come to the same conclusion: that participants believe this is a fair way to resolve disputes. Further, in actuality, most minor disputes are shunted aside or mass-processed by the judicial system in a way that provides very little of the first-class justice that is called for in fair and open adjudication through the courts (Goldberg, Green, & Sander 1986:293).

Mediated settlements involve a compromise of legal entitlements, which are particularly of concern when there are sharp power disparities between the disputing parties. As Goldberg and colleagues point out, the belief that legal protection is compromised is based on the assumption that many persons relegated to alternative processes would rather go to court. This does not appear to be the case when disputants have an ongoing relationship or the dispute involves a number of people. Mediation, in these instances, may be far more responsive to the needs of the disputants than adjudication (Goldberg, Green, & Sander, 1986:293).

Coercion in and into Mediated Settlements

The criticism related to difficulties in exacting consensus from feuding parties in the conciliation process also includes the problems in coercing them to adhere to the final agreements. The coercive role of the criminal justice system cannot be matched in informal justice centers. To compensate, some programs have come to rely on the courts as a threat to disputants, should one or both of the individuals abrogate an agreement. This involvement of the courts in providing incentive to maintain agreements creates a vexing problem to people involved in mediation, who pay lip service to its noncoercive principle. Elements of coercion are introduced, however, through court referrals, continuations of cases in court, and the fact that unsolved problems can and will be referred back to court (Merry, 1982a:179).

Roehl and Cook argue that coercion appears strongest in referrals by judges, where prosecution is real and not just threatened. They report that mediation takes place in 82 percent of the cases referred to judges as opposed to 14 percent to 22 percent in nonjustice referrals. Roehl and Cook maintain, however, that the high dropout rate (about 50 percent) in the majority of the programs indicates that most individuals do not seem to feel coerced by the threat of prosecution. In New York City Court (dealing with assault and harassment cases) one or both parties fail to appear in nearly two-thirds of the cases scheduled for mediation.

> We tend to agree...that as long as disputants are fully informed about the mediation process and alternatives, and can "exit the process" at will, low key intake coercion is not abhorrent but necessary until public awareness and acceptance grows. (Roehl & Cook, 1985:174)

Indeed, less than a third of the cases referred to Neighborhood Justice Centers (NJCs) by prosecutors, court clerks, and police officers were actually handled through mediation hearings (Roehl & Cook, 1985:174).

At the same time, some people argue that there is not enough coercion in the mediation process to make it a desirable alternative to disputants. Merry and Silbey (1984) point out that there is a recurring puzzle in the research on community mediation programs: a low rate of voluntary usage of alternatives despite extensive criticism of the public court's ability to handle problems with interpersonal dimensions. As Abel points out, on the face of it, mediators outnumber the mediated upon. Quite legitimately, he suggests, we should continue to question why it is that alternative dispute resolution concepts and symbols are so powerful and attractive yet so very difficult to implement (Abel, 1982:269).

Merry and Silbey suggest that citizens do not use alternatives voluntarily because by the time a conflict is serious enough to warrant third-party intervention, disputants do not want what alternatives have to offer. "At this point, the grievant wants vindication, protection of his or her rights (as he or she perceives them), an advocate to help in the battle, and a third party to uncover the 'truth' and declare the other party wrong" (Merry & Silbey, 1984:152). Before the escalation of the dispute, courts are the location of last resort, as most disputants prefer to handle problems by themselves.

The lack of coercion in mediation also raises some concern about the usefulness of this approach in dealing with anything other than minor criminal complaints. The public demand for punishment of "offenders," discussed in Chapter 4, serves to preclude the application of mediation to serious crime, even though we have seen that informal sanctions play an important role in enhancing deterrence. Mediation contributes to efforts made to reduce the conditions for escalation, which may result in violence and injury. Even then there are those who argue that mediation is the wrong approach in dealing with violent relationships, as in the case of family violence (Woods, 1985).

Leaving families to resolve problems of interpersonal violence themselves has been replaced by a new police mandate to intervene, using the weight of the law against the offender (male or female). The voices on the side of mediation argue that this policy leads to a breakdown of the family, with high risk for the individuals (most often the wife). The side for police intervention sees the benefits of the deterrent effect of arrest controlling future assaultive behavior of the offender (Sherman & Berk, 1984). Those who opt for no intervention (their numbers are getting smaller) search for a view of the family as self-regulating. Woods (1985) says that prosecutors, judges, and court administrators seek to use mediation both because of their belief that family violence is a private matter, and not a crime, and because they want to reduce their case loads. Rather than vigorously responding to family violence, which Woods argues would ultimately reduce the number of cases by reducing recidivism, they look to mediation to divert the cases from their calendars.

To Woods, mediation is both inappropriate and ineffective. "Not only does it fail to protect battered women but it is dangerous because it functions to perpetuate the violence" (Woods, 1985:6). This argument against mediation sees it as providing no sanctions to batterers. It seems wrong, however, to assume that charging wife batterers ensures that the action will not be repeated. What it does do, however, is to change the negotiation base of the offender with the victim. The arrest takes the quarrel into the court, altering the basis for informal sanctions of family and friends. This distinction is an important one because it allows us to argue that on-the-spot mediation may be inappropriate to deal with violence in the family but still recognize it as conflict-based and to be negotiated in court.

Mediation as a Tool for Community Cohesion

Mediation provides people with tools to help bring about desirable outcomes in dealing with disputes without invoking formal justice. This role of mediation—to educate the public concerning the rules of social processes—provides an important element of social control that is missing when individuals are left to sort out grievances on their own. As Merry (1982b) says, mediation could provide a means to counteract a state of anomie through the strengthening of social ties, especially in heterogeneous environments such as large urban centers. When tension develops between groups of different types, mediation could provide a means to discuss common problems and pose alternatives other than conflict to resolve difficulties.

Despite these problems, it is an oft-repeated sentiment that community mediation will revive the community structure and allow it to deal with disputes before they escalate to violence. This view is one that promotes the reduction of conflict through the conciliation of divergent viewpoints. According to Hofrichter, the approach to be adopted by Neighborhood Justice Centers is based on the assumption of a social order of harmonious values. It assumes that accommodation is desirable and the avoidance of serious controversy is an implicit goal (quoted in Tomasic, 1982:232). This removal of tension from communities may be attractive, but it ignores the fact that most often conflicts are dealt with through avoidance.

The desire to remove conflict from interpersonal relations is tied to a belief that we can recreate the community as it once appeared in smaller, homogeneous settlements. This includes the view that we can encourage the greater sharing of common values, setting an implicit standard for behavior that is acceptable to all parties. Merry (1982a) is critical of the current practice in mediation programs to remain value-free in judgments. The dilemma is that the disputants all pose their point of view in moral terms, justifying their own actions. When the mediators try to remove this moral tone from the proceedings, it tends to diminish the aspect of vindication that comes from settling a dispute in terms that are acceptable to both parties. Further, the assumption that both parties come to the dispute with equal claims ignores the fact that one of them may be in the wrong.

For mediation to play any role in the resolution of conflict that may have a criminal base, acknowledgment of moral wrongdoing may have to become an integral part of the mediator's position. This should be done if only to illustrate that there is a moral standard that has to be adhered to in society. The moral standard becomes evident in the ways in which the third party deals with the conflict.

This confusion of values and standards leads to a point at which a decision has to be made either to provide adjudication based on some agreed-upon principle or to mediate a compromise to reduce the tension but not deal with the source of the conflict. The clash of values that we see in our society clearly poses a serious problem for those who would seek to remove the tension that thereby arises. Realistically, the search for community that is developed in the mediation movement would succeed best in situations in which the mediators deliver services to people who are of the same background and experience. In fact, mediation efforts have failed when people of very different backgrounds have been brought together to resolve their differences through conciliation rather than through arbitration (Tomasic, 1982).

Further, Roehl and Cook argue that the pressure to use mediation programs as avenues of community change ignores their potential as specific alternatives to existing institutions of arbitration. That is, in response to those critics who say that mediation will work only if it is tied into an overall strategy of community change, Roehl and Cook reply that one can use mediation for the more modest goal of humanizing the court system (Roehl & Cook, 1985:171).

Mediation as Social Control

Abel (1982) states his case against mediation centers (Neighborhood Justice Centers) as an argument against the further extension of state power. Following this theme, Selva and Bohm argue that informal control extends beyond the most visible locations of state control, for example, courts, prisons, and mental hospitals, to permeate society at large. Appearing benign, these invisible systems increase the range of behavior subject to control. "In this way, the state reaches behavior that it would not be able to directly regulate by formal law" (Selva & Bohm, 1987:53). Although this position may be an overstated view of political control, the essence of the criticism is that individuals are increasingly encouraged to use forums other than the courts—collections of friends, family, and neighbors—to resolve conflict. The professionalization of conflict management, then, discourages individuals from taking their own position or of pursuing their rights informally, creating the possibility that conflict management is no longer possible without institutional intervention. The conflict that was appropriated by lawyers (Christie, 1977) now becomes appropriated by mediation professionals.

Responding to this criticism, Roehl and Cook argue that the fear that mediation expands state control and denies due process stems more from political philosophy than from empirical evidence. They believe that with appropriate safeguards on confidentiality, decision control, and the right to turn to the courts if necessary, undue state expansion appears to be a minimal risk (Roehl & Cook, 1985:175).

Further, as we pointed out, the problem of escalation may force people to choose either to involve the police where they are unwanted or to avoid the conflict entirely. The reality of the situation is that when individuals have access to agents, such as landlords or the police, they will try to use these resources to resolve conflict, especially in public disputes such as those between neighbors. When the situation is more private, the conflict is more likely to be handled through self-help, with neither formal nor informal agencies brought in. The dilemma that we face in our discussion of conflict management or resolution is that although we see the advantages of letting people solve their own problems through self-help, it can pose problems of retaliation and revenge, which enter into the domain of formal law. People seeking revenge are people out of control (Jacoby, 1983).

Clients of Mediation

Community mediation programs have gotten into trouble over the issue of who they serve and how well they serve them. These programs are most often offered in areas of low socioeconomic status. Further, when mediation programs are used for referral, they do not address the problems of access to the justice system but rather its inability or unwillingness to deal with problems faced by these low-income clients.

The attractiveness of informal institutions to authorities, Abel argues, is the fact that formal institutions often intervene only after patterns of deviant behavior have been firmly established. Informal justice provides the bases on which earlier state intervention can work to identify and correct situations of predelinquency, predeviance, and preconflict (Abel, 1982: 273). This fact has particular importance, in a negative way, because informal social control, as is the case with formal justice, is directed against the economically, socially, and politically oppressed. This bias, Abel maintains, is demonstrated by the fact that the Neighborhood Justice Centers are most likely to service individuals from lower socioeconomic areas.

The isolation of individuals from their natural group in the expression of grievances in mediation is also of concern to Abel (1982). He focuses on the fact that disputes are individualized, leaving structural deficiencies in the environment out of the solution. This inability to include the concerns of others in supporting one's claim reduces the effectiveness of mediation in bringing about solutions. Further, the inability to reduce the structural aspects in the environment (such as high density, landlord-tenant conflict, high transiency, high unemployment) leaves the disputes to be treated in individualistic rather than aggregate terms. This reluctance of mediators to get involved with disputes between the complainant and third parties constrains the mediator from attending to the underlying causes of the dispute (Felstiner & Williams, 1982).

Cavanagh and Sarat agree that mediation may provide an opportunity for communities to respond to conflict and to come together in solving it. However, merely substituting one publicly sponsored dispute resolution forum for another (i.e., public courts) will hardly be enough to reawaken a moribund spirit of community:"...the patient may be rendered more comfortable but his disease is not closer to a cure" (Cavanagh & Sarat, 1980:401). As Tomasic concludes, far from confronting the social structural causes of disputes, community mediators seem merely to induce disputants to accept the structural inequities that confront them (Tomasic, 1982:223). Again, this state of affairs may not be a damning criticism of the mediation movement if its intentions are to deal with conflict that arises out of inequity rather than with the inequity itself.

Abel's (1982) criticism of informal justice seems mostly focused on the centers that have sprung up in the last decade in the United States and Canada. The question is whether the criticisms that he, Merry (1982a), and others direct at mediation as currently practiced make this form of informal justice impossible to implement fairly, servicing all the concerns of citizens. Most especially, do the concerns that are expressed take a back seat to the overall problem that without these forms of mediation we will evolve to a level of social disorder accompanied by high crime rates? What is not clear is how the movement toward mediation has affected our experience with crime or with our attitudes toward the ways in which crime should be handled.

SUMMARY

I find it surprising that mediation programs have had support in a climate that calls for more law enforcement and more punishment. It is possible that their continued existence is ensured by their tie into the criminal justice system through referral. In addition, their persistence may be attributable to their ability to deal with more than just the symptoms of conflict. They establish an outlet for the discussion of larger issues than can be covered in a court of law. In addition, the support that mediation centers have received from the legal profession and the police indicates some level of acceptance of the idea that not all social conflict (even that of a criminal nature) can be handled in legalistic ways.

Edelman (1984) has written that the experience with mediation in the last decade has pointed to many problems with the institutionalized form of conflict management offered. He argues that the "first-stage" models are unlikely to be widely replicated, partly because of these problems and partly because of a disinclination to spend more money on what have proved to be expensive programs. What the first-stage models have provided, however, is the impetus to consider "second-stage" models, which build on the idea of mediation but operate in different ways.

These second-stage models include multi-door courthouses, which provide mediation and arbitration options within the courts themselves. This provision of resources can be coupled with a change in the legal structure, which legislates mediation when it is seen to have greater benefit than adjudication, as in child custody cases (Edelman, 1984:143). This legislation will not come into being without great controversy, but introducing the idea of mediation may lead to a quite different approach to definitions of how the court is to use its resources to maintain social order.

This change may actually come through an alteration in the attitudes of the professionals, already being seen in the area of corporate law. Rather than pursuing litigation, steps are being taken to encourage disputing companies to search for other means to resolve their conflicts. These alternatives include such things as mini-trials, where lawyers for each side make their arguments, without the rules of evidence, in front of executives from each side who have the authority to settle the case. The trial is presided over by a neutral adviser, who is there to provide assistance with the agreement terms (*New York Times*, 1986a:D2). Although the savings in money and time for the corporations is clearly an incentive to follow such a practice, it is not widespread; however, the logic of following such a procedure makes it attractive.

Whether or not the involvement of lawyers in the corporate area will spill over to new ways of making community mediation work on a larger scale in the area of criminal and civil law is still to be determined. The pressures that existed in the first-stage models are still there. The success of the mediation effort in overcoming the difficulties it has encountered over the last decade may rest on the ability to assimilate mediation into the ongoing work of the court. If assimilation occurs, the change in the attitude of the criminal justice system—to seeing crime as deriving from conflicts that can be resolved—may provide a dramatic reversal in the way in which we think about crime and crime prevention.

CHAPTER 6

Police and Informal Justice

INTRODUCTION

It seems a contradiction to discuss the role of the police in administering informal justice. Isn't their job, after all, to enforce the law? They are the guardians of formal justice. They are constrained by formal law. Law limits what they can use to contain and control deviant behavior in society. They are organized in hierarchical, quasi-militaristic organizations that promote conformity and strict adherence to rules and codes of behavior. They work to detect and punish criminality. Yet, as we will see in this chapter, the police make extensive use of informal or discretionary acts of coercion. To operate efficiently on a day-to-day basis, the police must be able to get community support for maintaining order and reducing conflict that escalates to crime.

Often the police are called on to make decisions about the best way to manage situations in which arrest is really only one of a number of alternatives. Negotiation, conciliation, or mediation are viable options for the police to deescalate conflict. Recognizing the conflict nature of crime, the police are put into the role of choosing between defining a grievance as one in which formal claim should be made or one in which informal action, either by the police or the victim, is more appropriate.

In this chapter, we will examine how the police have conventionally approached dispute resolution. We will then turn to specific examples of conflict-based policing to illustrate the role that the police must take in dealing with these problems. This discussion includes examining the elements of discretion, or selective enforcement of law, which set the boundaries of criminality through negotiation. The importance of police culture and organizational structure will be considered, as will experiments with forms of community involvement in policing. We can begin with an analysis of the concepts of deterrence versus coercion in governing the strategies that police use in maintaining social order.

POLICE ORIENTATION TO LAW AND ORDER

Compliance versus Deterrence-based Policing

Wilson (1983) points out that the original mandate for the police was maintenance of order. In the early days of North American history, solving crimes was a private matter and only later became incorporated into the activity of municipal police forces. Order maintenance or the **compliance** role of the police was coterminous with "community relations." The police were to protect the community from disorderly behavior—reducing conflict where they found it (Monkkonen, 1983). As Klockars states, the police are not "law-enforcement" agencies but "regulatory" institutions. Their job, as they practice it, is not to enforce the laws but to regulate relationships between people (Klockars, 1985:106–107).

Reiss (1984) states that the principal objective of compliance law enforcement is to secure conformity with the law by resorting to means that induce that conformity. Compliance systems seek to create law-abidingness and rely on preventive or remedial actions. This process does not necessitate the detection, processing, and penalizing of violators but rather emphasizes the need to provide incentives to individuals to comply with the law or to threaten to invoke penalties for noncompliance.

Compliance-based policing puts a different emphasis on what is seen as criminal. The focus on "noncrime" removes the police from the role of controlling crime to one of dealing with the roots of crime, often manifested in social conflict. It recognizes the necessity to enlist the efforts of the public in bringing about controls on social disorder both by reporting to the police and, further, by allowing the police to play the role of intermediary in community conflict (Lawson, 1982). What is noncrime is the residue from the process of identifying and classifying crime incidents (Mastrofski, 1983:37). The coercive activities of the police are treated as providing an informal, albeit discretionary, response to problems of disorder in the community.

The principal objective of **deterrence** law enforcement is to secure conformity with the law by detecting violations of it, identifying responsibility for violations, and penalizing perpetrators. Penalties are assessed to inhibit future violations both by the offender (specific deterrence) and by those who become aware of the punishment (general deterrence) (Reiss, 1984:91). The stated objectives of policing have increasingly emphasized the apprehension of offenders and the discretionary powers of police officers in making arrests and in gathering evidence (Reiss, 1984:84).

In contemporary times, the criminal law, as well as police managers and line officers, treat peacekeeping and order-maintenance functions as residual matters. Beyond the simple concern that real policing involves arrest, the problem for the police is that many compliance-based actions are without legitimation by police organizations and there is no training for compliance-based operations. As Mastrofski (1983:34) says, the crime-fighting and noncrime public service functions coexist uneasily in the police profession. The former dominate training curricula, career incentives, and organization evaluations, whereas the latter permeate the workload. Lawson (1982:157) points out that, except for traffic, most police officers actually spend little time in enforcement (10–15%). Rather, they are generally involved in keeping the peace and answering general assistance calls. This function has required the police to change from the role of "gladiator," which involves an image of crime fighter, to one of mediator, which projects the less desirable (to the police) image of conciliator or "social worker" (Lawson, 1982).

Types of Police Organizations

The police operate within organizational frameworks in which certain principles of action are considered acceptable and others are not. The hierarchical nature of the police force encourages members to operate according to a set of beliefs that are consistent with chains of command and a strong sense of obedience, leading to rigid conceptions of order (Skolnick, 1966). In terms of law enforcement, the emphasis falls on the rights of individual citizens, hence constraining the initiative of legal officials. There is a tension, then, between the organizational demands for order and the community's demands for legality.

As Smith (1984) explains, there are four types of police agencies. Their characterization is based on a matrix that includes, on the one side, bureaucratization, and on the other, professionalism (see Figure 6.1). For Smith, bureaucratization includes factors related to department size, number of occupational titles, and degree of vertical segmentation measured through the number of ranks. Professionalism includes the average education of the officers, the proportion of officers who have completed one year of education since joining the department, the mean number of years of schooling of officers since joining the department, and the proportion of officers with a college degree.

Bureaucratization

Professionalism		High	Low
	High	Legalistic	Service
	Low	Militaristic	Fraternal

Figure 6.1. Model of Police Organizations (Source: Adapted from Douglas Smith, "The Organization Context of Legal Control," *Criminology*, 22(1): 19–38.)

Put together, the levels of bureaucratization (from low to high) are cross-tabulated against the degree of professionalism (from low to high), yielding the four different categories of police agencies. These include non-professional groups with low complexity of bureaucracies, labeled **fraternal**; nonprofessional bureaucratic agencies, referred to as **militaristic**; **service** agencies, with high professionalization and low bureaucratization; and **legalistic** agencies, with high professionalism and high bureaucratization. These concepts are expanded on ideas borrowed from Wilson (1968), who argues that organizational style will affect interorganizational variation in law enforcement. Douglas Smith (1984) reports quite different responses in the ways in which the police handle arrests, depending on their organizational character.

In professional departments that are not bureaucratic, the style of control exercised in disputes is conciliatory, whereas in bureaucratic, nonprofessional police agencies disputes are often considered to be too minor to warrant involving the law. When the force is both bureaucratic and professional, officers tend to exercise more legal control.

> Increasing the bureaucratization of professional police agencies results in a shift from conciliatory to punitive social control of interpersonal disputes, while increasing the professionalism of bureaucratic police agencies places disputes within the legitimate domain of police work. (Douglas Smith, 1984:35)

The importance of these findings lies in what they tell us about the propensity of the police to reflect the character of the agency of which they are a part when handling interpersonal disputes and responding in legalistic or conciliatory ways. Not only must we be conscious of the belief systems of the police and their relationship with the community in bringing about social order, but we must also consider how the goals and structure of the organization facilitates the development of certain strategies of crime control. The internal reward system for crime fighting as opposed to community liaison can be a major impediment in certain forces to getting involved in negotiation strategies for maintaining social order. The means of assessing achievement can be at odds with the community's needs. Further, the demands for law enforcement with no discretion on the part of the officer can come from outside of the force, restricting the police from getting involved in these community activities.

POLICE DISCRETION

Law and Order

The coexistence of deterrence-based law enforcement and a compliance model gives us a way of looking at the negotiation of the boundaries of illegality that the police define in interaction with the public. As Reiss (1984) points out, a legal standard generally recognizes only some threshold of risk in allowing certain behavior to occur without the need for sanction to prevent harm. The tests of this threshold of compliance can vary in their precision. As a result, the less precision there is in measuring compliance and ensuring deterrence through arrest, the more discretion a law enforcement agent has to determine compliance.

> Moreover, the more tests than an agent has at his disposal to determine the level or threshold of compliance, the more the agent is open to negotiation of what constitutes compliance. Thus the determination of what is compliance generally rests in the social construction and reconstruction of reality by control agents and by those they seek to control. (Reiss, 1984:93)

Given the popular view that the police must adhere closely to the law in their work, it may seem surprising to some readers that they use discretion in deciding whom to arrest. This discretion has been studied at some length by Black, who says that the police decision to give official recognition to a crime is ordinarily an outcome of face-to-face interaction between the police and the complainant rather than a programmed response to a bureaucratic or legal formula (Black, 1980:69). Thus, even where there is a complainant, the police may decide not to act on the complaint. When police encounter a dispute to which there is no obvious complainant, they may use strategies other than arrest to solve the problem.

Affecting this process are complaints that Mastrofski labels as having the greatest "crime potential." Officers, he claims, believe that incidents with certain characteristics have a far greater crime-fighting payoff than others. A citizen's robbery complaint may be treated as having great crime

potential even if the officer finally classifies it as an noncrime dispute between two drunken individuals. Alternatively, a routine neighbor complaint that ultimately results in an arrest may have initially been treated as
a minor dispute with no likelihood of law violation (Mastrofski, 1983:38).

Reiss (1984) suggests that what works well for the police often cannot
be permitted under the law. The coercive aspects of law enforcement often
require the police to use greater levels of discretion than may be acceptable
to the public. The enforcement remains informal, as a result, operating
outside of the control of police agencies, who feel that they cannot officially
condone this action.

As Klockars (1985) has argued, despite the illegality of selective enforcement and the power it puts into the hands of police officers, it is
required because of the overreach of the law. However, again, the police
agencies feel that they cannot officially acknowledge this discretion. What
this means, then, is that the police agencies are unable to develop internal
policies to control abuses in selective enforcement.

Although not condoning this aspect of selective enforcement, police
forces have become more aware of the community's concerns, outlining
the standards with which they can maintain order while staying within the
boundaries of legality. The concern for order must not impede the administration of the law and vice versa. The example of this tension between law
and order is illustrated by Skolnick's example that it would be a violation
of the rule of law for a legislature to make epilepsy a crime even though a
seizure typically upsets public order (Skolnick, 1966:9).

The tension between law and order is made more complex, Skolnick
(1966) points out, because there is often ambiguity in the application of the
law. There are varying definitions of what is acceptable behavior under the
law. Sometimes it is difficult, if not impossible, for the legislature, through
the courts, to take away all discretion from the police in their handling of
conflict in the community. The discretion that is exercised may lead to a
lessening of legal sanctions in exchange for order. This result is often seen
in cases of crowd control when drug use may be flagrant but remains un-
sanctioned. Charging individuals will lead to strong reaction, even by those
in the crowd who are not involved in drug use. The disruption involved in
upsetting the crowd offsets the value of enforcing the drug laws.

In addition, the police rely heavily on the disputants or observers to
bring disputes to their attention. They often respond, then, in a reactive
rather than proactive fashion (Black, 1980:68). That is, the police react to
situations where they are asked for assistance or where there is a clearly
defined victim. This fact causes difficulties in maintaining constant social
order and in providing consistent responses to criminal behavior that may
occur in a community but is undetected by the police. Further, in cases
of social conflict in which the antagonists may be of equal standing, they

are intimately related, or there is some sense that the parties are able to take care of their own problems, the police may simply choose to ignore the situation. Such a choice keeps disputants from entering the criminal justice system.

Skolnick (1966) has referred to "justice without trial" as the application of enforcement outside of the normal procedure of the courts, which the police see as an important aspect of their attempt to maintain order. The use of discretionary powers to arrest in some cases and not in others is an example of the way in which justice without trial can work. When discretion is removed from the police,[1] they would argue that they may lose control over a situation in which conflict may be reduced in other ways. Proponents of the mandatory charge option argue that the police should not be given the opportunity to judge which cases are right for arrest and which are not. The police assessment, the critics argue, may be based on factors that go beyond the assault, such as the offender's demeanor (Visher, 1983).

Smith and Klein (1984) report that police responses to problematic situations reflect a number of considerations beyond the lawfulness of behavior. How police decide to handle such problems—we would say that these are problems on the borders of crime—reflect normative and practical considerations, a point first made by Bittner (1967).

> For example, police response to interpersonal disputes may be influenced by the relationship between disputing parties, whether anyone has been hurt, whether physical violence has occurred, the complainant's request for specific police action, and prior knowledge of the disputants by the police. (Smith & Klein, 1984:468)

Police decision making, then, is affected both by legal considerations and situational exigencies. Police can arrest, remove one party from the scene, attempt to settle the argument, or simply do nothing at all (Smith & Klein, 1984:468).

In a study done in Norwalk, Connecticut, Bard and Zacker (1976) report that police officers frequently use mediation as a way of reducing conflict between disputants. Reflecting back to Skolnick's (1966) distinction between adherence to the law and maintenance of social order, we see the need for police discretion as a way of maintaining order, even if it means not adhering strictly to the law.

---

[1] As it has been, for example, in family violence cases and in the recently implemented program of Zero Tolerance, used to confiscate property at border points when drugs or drug paraphenalia are found on individuals being searched.

Discretion in Dealing with Family Violence

The problems that the police have in dealing with family violence illustrate the dilemma that faces them in dealing with interpersonal disputes on the borders of crime. The debate centers on whether or not the police should arrest the offender when arrest may not actually deal with the root of the family conflict and may in fact heighten it so that is becomes even more dangerous. With the redrawing of the lines of criminality to include many cases of domestic violence that before were left to the family members themselves, we find that the police role is growing. Even so, it is still unclear whether or not arrest will solve the problems encountered in the family, despite reducing the overt incidence of these events. In addition, police involvement in the first place cannot be taken for granted. Dutton (1987) reports that in Vancouver, during a six-month study period, police attended only 54 percent of the reported cases of husband-wife dispute.

Research recently completed in Minnesota indicates there are strong deterrent effects with mandatory arrest procedures in place (Sherman & Berk, 1984). However, as Berk and Loseke explain, the decision to arrest or not directs attention away from the routine exercise of police discretion. "Police interpretations of the situation, their prior experience, and situation-specific rationales for decisions are all inherent in the policing enterprise" (Berk & Loseke, 1980–81). Faced with mandatory arrest procedures, the police must still include information in their evaluation of the situation that may preclude arrest. Police forces must also deal with the reality that even when arrest is required, if the officers do not believe in its efficacy, they will not proceed if there is any element of doubt attached to the case (Berk et al., 1982).

A factor in determining the role of the police in controlling family violence relates to the deterrence that occurs when individuals recognize that these acts are criminal and will be treated as such by the police. The arrest option provides specific deterrence effects, and the example that charging sets for others may provide general deterrence. Further, as Sherman explains,[2] there may be a strong effect realized by the return of the police to the scene of previous violence. The fact that people engage in violence because they feel that it is acceptable and they can get away with it may be dealt with by creating a police presence. Further, Sherman reports the interesting finding that an important factor in deterring future violence involves whether or not a police officer (according to the victim) took the time to listen to the victim's story before taking action. "When the officers reportedly listened to the problems, the deterrent effect was enhanced;

---

[2] Personal communication.

when they did not, the deterrent effect was greatly reduced" (Sherman, 1984:67).

With the new policies requiring a police charge, when before the onus was on the victim of family violence, the officer is faced with the decision about whether sufficient grounds exist for making the charge stick. This decision is further complicated by police concerns that further problems might occur in the family as a result of this action. There is also an over-riding belief that the violence will be driven further underground by the threat of court-imposed sanctions.

The trepidation with which the police approach domestic violence derives from the potentially hazardous nature of these calls. In addition, the frustration that comes from the fact that the victims are often unwilling to cooperate or are likely to return to the home after the incident makes the police skeptical of the effectiveness of their intervention. Further, police officers feel that they are not social workers and should not be relied on to provide mediation or counseling in these situations. As Sherman and Berk (1984) suggest, the police themselves would favor forced separation as a means of achieving short-term peace. The problem can then be dealt with by others in the community whose job it is to counsel people with these problems, leaving the police to get on with their job of "fighting crime."

Obviously, the police have been thrust into the role of mediators by circumstances—sometimes promoted by new training programs in response to the problems regularly encountered by untrained officers faced with domestic conflict (see Reiss, 1984:106). The rejection of mediation as an alternative strategy in cases of severe family violence forces the police to drop all discretion when there is proof of bodily harm. The process whereby we have gone from (1) ignoring these problems to (2) demanding mediation from police to (3) mandatory charging provides an interesting backdrop to our assessment of the ways in which we have changed in our views of conflict and our responses to it. This change includes a demand to criminalize family violence when we become aware of its costs to victims and to the society at large. There is a sense in which experiments in police practice, such as that reported in the Minnesota family violence research, comes to be dominated by a deterrence rather than a compliance model (Reiss, 1984).

> The issue addressed in these experiments is a determination of the effect that arrest has as a deterrent. The problem could just as easily be formulated to ask what kind of police practice, if any, might prevent spouse assault from occurring. (Reiss, 1984:106)

The police cannot be expected to deal with the problem of family violence on their own. It is clear that the community's response to family violence and the actions of the police must interact to ensure any success in dealing effectively with this social problem. As has been found in the Minnesota Domestic Abuse Intervention Project operating out of Duluth, the most important aspect in changing the criminal justice system's response to wife battering is the need to coordinate the many actors to secure a consistent and uniform response. Policies that promote arrest and increase convictions, actions that place legal constraints on assailants and increase their incarceration, directives that require treatment for violent behavior and when necessary protect victims from further contact with the assailant are all effective only when they are uniformly applied (Pence, 1985:9). Key actors in the related areas of social services, medicine, education, and the ministry who come into contact with these problems must be able to join the effort to deal with them effectively.

Mediation may occur, then, through the police use of existing social service agencies in the community on a referral basis. Palenski (1984) says that the use of mediation services by the police would seem to provide them with several advantages. First, it gives them an alternative method in handling family disputes. Second, it could give them a means to divert criticism of their handling of interpersonal conflict to a neutral agency, hence reducing the public's hostility to their intervention in personal matters.

Third, mediation gives the police the chance to reduce their involvement in the area's interpersonal problems, leaving them to concentrate more heavily on the more "central" aspects of policing, that is, detecting and controlling crime. This leads to a fourth reason for using mediation— the opportunity it provides to improve managerial capabilities. The police can allocate their resources more effectively, relying on the mediation programs to control the conflict that emerges in family and neighborhood confrontations. Finally, participation by the police in mediation efforts can help strengthen police-community ties. In handling domestic disputes, the police may be seen as indifferent, unresponsive, and ineffective. Promoting mediation may help improve the view the public has of police activity and performance (Palenski, 1984:33).

The reality of the situation is that police rarely use the mediation programs that exist in the community. Although the police are seen as important for the referral of cases to these programs, the police are excluded in the organizations' planning. Thus the programs are not as responsive to police needs, nor are they seen as being a predictable force in resolving the problems of referred individuals.

Police Clients and Discretion

Generally, a number of factors can influence the decision that the police make in enforcing legal sanctions. These include decisions about the relationship of antagonists, the attitude of the antagonists toward the police, the tolerance of the community for certain types of conflict, the relationship that the police develop in dealing with community institutions to bring about order, and the structure of the police organization. When the police take on a "ministerial" role, they usurp the power of the magistrate in the court (Rumbart & Bittner, 1979:242).

Smith and Klein report from their study of police intervention in domestic and nondomestic disputes that, as suggested by Black (1980), one of the most significant determinants of arrest was the complainant's preference for arrest. This factor was contingent, however, on the socioeconomic status (SES) of the neighborhood in which the dispute occurred. As the SES of neighborhoods increase, so does the likelihood that the police will go along with the request for arrest even when the officers prefer not to charge (Smith & Klein, 1984:477). Douglas Smith (1987) reports further that the police are more likely to arrest and less likely to mediate disputes in low-status neighborhoods. Prior police knowledge of complainants can lead them to act with indifference to a complaint; however, repeated experience with disputes between the same people can lead to greater likelihood of arrest.

Important in affecting arrest decisions are the predisposition and values of the police officers, which can be a function of the beliefs they have of their role in the community. Officers may find certain individuals more credible and may decide that certain strategies work best in certain situations even when a specified course of action is required by law. Important in affecting this attitude is the demeanor of the offenders toward the police. Antagonistic offenders are more likely to be arrested. In addition, if there is a belief that the incident will recur, for example if alcohol is present, the police are more likely to make an arrest to prevent future conflict (Smith & Klein, 1984:479).

Characteristics of offenders have also been shown to affect decisions to arrest. Arrest is more likely in disputes in which males are involved. Visher argues that traditional patterns of interaction between men and women (determined by notions of "chivalry") influences the formal sanctioning of female offenders. Females who meet the criterion of proper demeanor and fit the middle-class view that the police have of acceptable behavior from women receive lenient and preferential treatment. "Discretion in the criminal justice system involving female offenders appears related to notions of chivalry and bargaining relationships" (Visher, 1983:23).

Some individuals do not want to involve the police in their disputes because they see these conflicts as private. This avoidance process can cause real problems for the police in getting a case in to court. The police must question the value of arrest when there is an expectation that the individuals (especially those who are intimate) could bring about a solution to the conflict through their own resources better than could be achieved through the courts.

POLICE CULTURE: ATTITUDES TOWARD
CLIENTS AND THE CRIMINAL JUSTICE SYSTEM

There is a police culture that gives the police beliefs about what to expect in certain situations and prescribed, albeit informal, ways of dealing with them. It could be argued that this police culture views minor community disputes as noncrime, that is, as problems of order maintenance, which would mean that these problems are treated lightly. However, this belief does not seem to borne out by Mastrofski's research. He reports that although investigation is more likely to take place for crime versus non-crime activity, assistance and coercion are used as frequently for noncrime activities, such as disputes, as for cases of violent crime (Mastrofski, 1983:44). So despite a police culture that acts to downplay intervention of this sort, it does take place and is a means of defusing situations that may become violent or criminal. This precrisis intervention, or "prophylactic" approach, suggests that police efforts to thwart crime should focus more on prevention and less on response to reports of crimes that have already occurred (Mastrofski, 1983:45).

The practice of involving the community in helping to maintain social order may be confounded by the influence of the belief system of police, who often see the citizenry as hostile toward them. They see themselves as conservative, both emotionally and politically. Isolated from the community that they serve (Mastrofski, 1983:63), they respond with clannishness and loyalty to one another (Mastrofski, 1983:59). In addition, they often see themselves as at odds with the justice system of which they are a part. For example, for procedural reasons, the system occasionally releases individuals that the police are convinced are guilty—which leads to police frustration.

Police are also annoyed by the unwillingness of citizens to help them do their job or to prosecute their assailants when they have been caught or charged. According to Skolnick, when the tension between police beliefs and those of the community increase, the police are more likely to lean toward an arbitrary invocation of authority to achieve what they perceive to be the goals of criminal law. "Along with these effects is an elevation of crime control to a position where it is valued more than the principle of accountability to the rule of law" (Skolnick, 1966:11). In other words, when there is some ambiguity in the application of the law, police officers will apply their own conception of order. In this way, the police, who see their role as one of reducing conflict, may in fact be acting to enhance it.

This conflict may be aggravated by public hostility because of the police officers' role as law enforcers, sometimes confounded through a lack of understanding of the community in which they are operating. The problems of ethnic and racial tension between the police and certain minority groups has led to many forces actively recruiting from these groups. This recruitment is to ensure that the community members do not react to policing in a negative fashion because of a perception that the police represent majority group beliefs and interests (see Klein, Thomas & Bellis, 1971).

Wilson reports on studies that indicate that the police do not, in fact, attract general hostility from large segments of urban populations. However, there is resentment directed toward them by select groups, most often young males (Wilson, 1983:92). More important for successful police-community relations are their efforts to develop a system of communication with community members, ranging from the simple presence of police officers on foot patrols to active involvement in community policing efforts.

NEW ATTEMPTS TO INTRODUCE OLD IDEAS: NEIGHBORHOOD POLICING STRATEGIES

The police must rely on community members to support them in their efforts to bring about order. This effort can, at times, include the use of self-help, as discussed earlier. Or it can take the form of coproduction, in which the police use members of the community as supporters of their activity (Krahn & Kennedy, 1986). Coproduction can include passive responses, such as locking doors, to more active ones, such as participation in crime-prevention programs or working as an informant (Skolnick, 1966). As Black (1980) points out, since the typical criminal act occurs at a specifically unpredictable time and place, the police must rely on citizens to involve them in the average case. Most often the citizen who calls the police is a victim of a crime who seeks justice in the role of complainant.

An example of the impact of the contrast in police and community beliefs is provided by the riots that occurred in London in the summer of 1981. The Brixton riots, according to the Scarman inquiry appointed by the government to look into the reasons for the upheaval, could be clearly traced to "Operation Swamp" (Scarman, 1981). In this operation, the police targeted certain areas in the London suburb for sweeps and selective searches. These "attacks" on the areas were seen as highly provocative by the local community and disruptive of normal social control. In their defense, the police argued that this program was the only way to ensure that predatory crime was contained in the area.

The Scarman inquiry was highly critical of such a form of policing. It came out strongly in favor of a community policing strategy that would more closely link police with community leaders in working out crime-control mechanisms in the area. The police were encouraged to consult more broadly with the leaders in the community to reduce the tension within groups as well as between the public and the police, to ensure that there would not be a recurrence of major social upheaval (Alderson, 1985).

Community service policing has been tried in a number of jurisdictions with differing levels of success. At the heart of the concept of neighborhood team policing is the long-term assignment of officers to a particular area. This continuity in appointment and the delegation of broader authority to take action that may go beyond the strict definition of the police role provide a greater sensitivity to community needs and a greater awareness of community problems. However, these programs have met resistance from police managers who see decentralization as limiting their control over their officers (Scheingold, 1984:134). The demands of the hierarchy for aggressive patrol tactics while officers are trying to establish a rapport with the public can make this form of community-based policing confusing to the officers, thereby reducing its effectiveness (Scheingold, 1984:135). Where departments do not encourage this activity, many officers will simply opt to ignore it. Finally, officers become confused about the police role. Fear of being indecisive or being placed in the middle of a dispute may cause many officers to play the role of restoring order rather than acting as peacemaker (Palenski, 1984:35).

The development of crime-prevention and victim-service programs has further confused this picture because of the separation of these duties from regular policing, where they are seen to be performed by "social workers" in the force rather than police officers. This attitude has made it difficult for the regular force to integrate all its members into the role of community policing as a general crime-prevention strategy.

Organizational constraints also play a role in restricting the use of community-based policing strategies. Police budgets depend on case load, and referral to outside programs may create an impression of lower activity, hence lower budgets. Using alternative programs inserts the police into a broader struggle in defining their role in the community and in getting resources to realize their objectives. Although the police attempt to maintain political neutrality, it is very difficult for them to stay outside of the political arena when fighting for budget allocations as well as arguing for certain policing strategies.

For example, in a recent case in western Canada, when confronted with the possibility of cutbacks in the budget, the police department threatened to remove Barney the Bear, a part of a major outreach program in teaching crime prevention in the schools. The uproar against this cut, led by a five-year-old child, politicized the police budget debate. It offered a choice to the electorate to confront crime control alone or pay a bit more for community outreach as well.

Skogan's (1987) research on disorder in a number of major American cities suggests that there is real benefit from opening informal channels of communication between the public and the police. He outlines four approaches to community policing that he believes are worth implementing: (1) foot patrol, in which officers can make day-to-day contact with merchants and residents in specified areas; (2) storefront offices, which provide centers of proactive neighborhood operations; (3) community organizing, in which officers work with local specialists and community organizations to help guide the policing effort; and (4) team policing, in which groups of police are decentralized from headquarters into areas where they work to meet local community needs.

It has been argued that the effort to create community policing is especially appropriate in small towns, where the police have access to limited resources and where there is little opportunity to provide special service units, such as those used in London, Ontario, to deal with domestic problems (Jaffe & Burris, 1984). As Wilson points out, people living in small towns are more tolerant of police actions to control crime than are those living in large cities. Wilson speculates that this attitude may be due to a sense of greater collaboration between these individuals and the police in fighting crime, whereas people in big cities request and receive police services on an individual basis (Wilson, 1983:86). The prospects for big-city community policing are positive but need to be seen as operating best in small local areas, where the police can have maximum impact. These programs will clearly not be as successful if they are imposed on all parts of the city indiscriminately.

The community policing concept allows the police to deal with social problems and crime by coordinating major actors in the community. The experiments with community policing in Britain have demonstrated that although the police must enforce the law, they require the resources of the community to identify areas of need and to deal with problems that go beyond the resources available to the police (Moore & Brown, 1981). Attempts have been made by police departments to use community committees as a forum for the discussion of social problems and as a means of airing concerns about enforcement.

The most important role of the community group is to act as a vehicle for the promotion of intervention programs and to set up a mechanism whereby individuals faced with violence who are afraid to call in the police have an alternative to turn to, such as social services or mediation programs. When serious violence is encountered, the police can then be called in. Individuals may also be advised about the alternatives available to them. The key for this community committee is to be a clearing house of available services and resources.

For these programs to work there has to be a reconciliation of the role of police as enforcers (as this surely stays an important part of their job) with the police as members of the community who act to prevent crime through negotiation and mediation of local problems. As Shaffer explains in her discussion of community policing programs in Britain, the more the community members get to know the police officers as individuals who are concerned and sympathetic as well as controlling and disciplining, the more chance there will be of improving communication and cooperation between the police and the public. "Policing in a democratic society is impossible without this co-operation" (Shaffer, 1980:38).

SUMMARY

It is apparent from this discussion that the police need to move back to a posture of maintaining order instead of strictly fighting crime. This move means that they will be increasingly called on to respond to disputes and conflict with mediation or conciliation. This idea has created some difficulty for police as they have seen that the legalistic approach to crime fighting by the legislatures and the courts has removed their discretion to maintain order through extralegal means. In addition, the organizational structure of certain police forces makes it difficult for officers to operate in the community in a mediative way. They get few rewards for community programs. Even where these programs are put in place, they are often the first to be cut when budgets get tight and the demand for police on the street has greater priority.

The call for more citizen involvement in reducing conflict and fighting crime comes with an increase in pressure on the police to use less discretion in adjudicating cases they encounter in their daily work. More discretion for the police may mean more order (although not necessarily so). But it may also mean less justice. Less discretion may expand the boundaries of crime to include conflict normally dealt with in other ways.

The success of the police action may rest in reducing hostility between the police and the community through the more direct inclusion of the public in crime prevention. Support may range from passive participation, simply protecting oneself from harm, to active involvement in community crime-prevention programs. The intervention of the public in reducing conflict may also take on the character of vigilantism, although a compromise position that sets out clear guidelines for the involvement of the public in disputes may be possible.

It is surprising how the different sides of this issue are lining up. Where we would expect support for community involvement we find fear of the loss of individual justice. Where we would expect the support of individual choice, we find a concern for the implications it has for collective order. The middle ground sees community support of policing as serving to reduce conflict. This view is important for the development of means to remove the areas of tension that lead to the decay of interpersonal relations supporting a revival of community responsibility for the maintenance of social order.

Wilson (1983) complains about the lack of police options provided by sociological theories of crime, characterizing them as being unable to pose solutions to the problem without calling for major changes in the structure of society. Here we have a logical base for the attack on crime that involves simple changes in the bureaucratic and political structure of policing. Some of these changes are underway now, driven by the day-to-day pressures of police activity. To keep the momentum going, we need to impart a rationale for this approach. It seems most clearly to rest in the understanding of the ways in which crime is connected to social conflict and the need for community-based approaches to reduce the incidence of conflict.

The police response will lead to a change in emphasis from solving crime to resolving conflicts. This may become a positive force in filling the void left by the difficulties encountered in the mediation programs, which have found that clientele are reluctant to use their services, partly it seems because of the ineffectiveness of the sanctions they offer. To incorporate the police as one group of actors in the mediation process, and to include the community members more directly in ongoing discussions of sources of conflict, seems a realistic direction to go in bringing about the integration of these now separate efforts. (Despite the referral of individuals to mediation programs, this is an insignificant part of police practice.)

Many would say that it is unrealistic to promote community involvement in a highly mobile, segmented society. And yet it is exactly this mobility and segmentation that causes the conflict. The reasonable expectation that conflict will lessen when informal ties develop between individuals, and agents of control are available to provide sanction when conflict heats up, seems an important step to take in realizing some success in our fight against crime.

The police have to take the initiative to incorporate into their organizational structures viable alternatives to enforcement, much in the same way as the courts are recognizing their limitations in providing adjudicative dispute resolution exclusively. When these alternatives are given equal weight, their viability as ways of maintaining social order can be more fairly tested. As Reiss (1984:107) points out, in the absence of systematic testing of alternatives, one must base police training and practice on the folklore of police practice in peacekeeping. The police officer's tendency to respond to most disorder (or noncrime) in mediative ways must be matched by changes in the ways in which the police organizations process this activity. This step may narrow the boundaries of crime and provide a way in which noncrime can be kept from escalating into criminal behavior.

CHAPTER 7

Conflict Management and the Role of the Courts

INTRODUCTION

Warren Burger, the former chief justice of the U.S. Supreme Court, has argued that a major reason courts have become overburdened is that Americans are increasingly turning to formal justice for relief from a range of personal distresses and anxieties. Solutions for personal wrongs that were once seen as the responsibility of social institutions other than the courts are now promoted as legal "entitlements." "The courts have been expected to fill the void created by the decline of church, family, and neighborhood unity" (Burger, 1982:275). Burger calls for increasing use of "nonjudicial routes" in the resolution of disputes, including arbitration and negotiation. For such an influential figure in the legal community to opt for alternative justice, not only to unclog the courts but also to offer more humane alternatives to litigation, points out the importance of examining the role of the court to find its rightful place in solving disputes.

This chapter will examine the political and social pressures on courts to handle disputes of all kinds and the countervailing pressure within the system to transfer some of them to other forums, such as mediation. We will examine the roles that judges, prosecutors, and defense lawyers play in setting the stage for the introduction of alternatives—both within the system, through the use of such strategies as plea bargaining, and outside the system, through court-mandated arbitration. These roles provide important background in defining the justice system's response to conflict in communities.

COURTS AND CONFLICT MANAGEMENT

The Place of Courts in Managing Community Conflict

Courts filter disputes by carefully controlling their rules of access. The kinds of disputes that will be dealt with, who can bring them forward, and possible solutions determine the involvement of public, formal adjudicators in defining, managing, and interpreting conflict (Sarat & Grossman, 1975:1207). As Sarat and Grossman point out, in contrast to private, informal mechanisms, the "rules" for a decision in court do not come from the parties themselves. Rather they are laid out in statutes, prior decisions, and evolving policy considerations.

Conflict management is reactive. Court action is also reactive. Sarat (1976:342) says that most studies fail to place litigation into the context of the full range of dispute alternatives available in society. There is also the problem that courts cannot take affirmative steps to ensure that triggering incidents represent a broader universe of problems that the decisions will affect.

Courts cannot "self-start" (Cavanagh & Sarat, 1980:379). Rather than promoting certain behavior, they must respond to those disputes that come to them. Thus the courts are preclusive, which is reminiscent of the difficulties faced by the police in controlling disorder. It is true, however, that judges can highlight, through their treatment of the problems brought to them, areas of social concern that need to be addressed. They can then recommend alternative means of conflict resolution, such as diversion. However, although individual complainants can take comfort in the treatment they receive, others of their class or social group may still have unresolved claims. This particularistic problem-solving removes the political threat from the system. The use of class action suits has reversed this effect to some extent, but the individualistic nature of litigation has served to reduce the use of the courts as a way of addressing collective grievances deriving from community-based conflict (Sarat & Grossman, 1975).

Court procedures in North America, generally, are formal and public. They are narrow in their conception of relevance and opt for an "all or nothing" style of decision making. The demand for relevance to the court imposes constraints on the dispute. That is, disputants focus the definition of their conflict. As discussed in Chapter 3, the search for relevance may transform personal problems arising out of complex situations into disputes over questions of fact or competing interpretations of rules and rights (Sarat, 1976:340).

Judges are constrained not only when determining which party shall prevail but also when prescribing the form that redress will take (Cavanagh & Sarat, 1980:383). If cases come to court, they are generally serious.

Whereas the optimal goal of dispute resolution in informal settings is directed at the mutual satisfaction of the disputing parties (Sarat & Grossman, 1975), at the level of public, formal dispute settlement, through the use of courts, the emphasis falls more heavily on rights and duties.

Merry's analysis of dispute processing in urban neighborhoods found that disputants use the courts frequently, but rarely successfully, as a mode of settling disputes. Although courts are used where informal sanctions are absent, she argues, they cannot fill this vacuum effectively. Rather, courts operate as a potential sanctioning agent to intimidate one's opponent, serving as an alternative to such self-help mechanisms as street violence (Merry, 1979:919).

The threat of court action is used as a weapon by individuals to enhance their power and influence. Most often this means of resolving disputes is used between people who have limited contact and are unlikely to have sustained future relationships. Merry's point about the use of courts is consistent with the view offered by Galanter (1983) that few cases are finally adjudicated in the courts. Instead, in neighborhood conflict at least, the court is used to deescalate the problem through formal action, such as court sentencing.[1] Bargaining in the "shadow of the law" (Mnookin & Kornhauser, 1979) extends to the problems faced in communities where the recourse to other means of conciliation is limited. This impact of judicial "aura" is as important in considering the societal role of courts as is the effectiveness of juridical decision making (Cavanagh & Sarat, 1980:373).

For those cases that find their way into court, societal tension can be reduced through the example set by this resolution. As pointed out by Coser (1956), societies need mechanisms to reduce their internal tension. They look for safety valves. Litigation provides a safety valve for individuals confronted with conflict and left without informal recourse. Repeating the view concerning the role of the police, Sarat and Grossman argue that grievances (even those beginning in a dyadic and fairly private relationship), if not settled, may escalate into more intense and often more organized and widespread demands on the political system. Courts serve as a guide to disputing in society. The output of litigation serves to direct nonlitigious settlement of many similar disputes (Sarat & Grossman, 1975). Although it is not clear how many informal disputes exist in society (Galanter, 1983), there is some basis to believe that the disputing climate will be influenced by the models provided for solution by the courts.

The pursuit of adjudication may also come as a result of the demand

---

[1] This is consistent with the findings, presented in Chapter 3, that police and landlords are frequently used to resolve neighborhood disputes.

for third-party judgment, allowing for vindication or assignment of guilt. This use of formal courts to designate wrong, assign blame, and coerce conformity through punishment is seen as an integral part of our criminal justice system. It has led to an interesting paradox in our view of this system. On the one hand, we are concerned about the leniency the courts show toward individuals seen as threats to peace and good order in society. On the other hand, we are shocked by the growth of court-based conflict management, exemplified by the "litigation explosion."

The Litigation Explosion

There has recently been a great deal of talk in the media about the problem of "hyperlexis," or overuse of the courts to settle disputes (Galanter, 1983). This litigation explosion may be symptomatic of our frustration with the means available to us to provide our own solutions. Evidence of overuse, it is felt, is substantiated by an overabundance of lawyers drumming up work for themselves (as "ambulance chasers" working on contingency fees). Concern is raised further by "atrocity stories" reported in the media of unusual abuse of the justice system. The ambulance chasers seem to be small in number. Further, the atrocity stories are often unsubstantiated, forming part of the urban myths and legends that spring up in society (Galanter, 1983:64). In fact, the United States and Canada are less litigious per capita than are many other countries, including New Zealand and Australia.

    The myths of litigiousness are promoted by widely publicized cases in which juries provide large settlements to injured parties (many of which are later overturned by appeals courts) under conditions that are highly suspect. The example of the psychic who sued for loss of her psychic power after having a CAT scan is repeated as proof of the outlandish nature of these settlements. In fact, the psychic won her settlement, not on the loss of her psychic powers (although that is why she sued), but rather because the jurors believed that she developed an allergic reaction as a result of the treatment. They were instructed to ignore her complaint about the loss of psychic ability.

    Similar cases of what appear to be outrageous settlements have been misreported by the media, reinforcing the public view of the abuse of litigation (*Biddeford Journal Tribune*, 1986b). However, this concern about hyperlexis seems to be more broadly based, fed by an underlying fear within the community that we are no longer able to deal with our own problems, marking the decline of civility and morality. As McIntosh (1983) points out, changes in the social order beget conflict, some of which is transformed into political mobilization and participation in government institutions.

Because claims made upon government assume different forms that reflect the division of political labor fashioned by constitutional design, the state faces the challenge of how to respond to a nonconstant array of expectations and demands...and is engaged in an ongoing process of dispute management. (McIntosh, 1983:991).

These demands can be translated into use of the courts. As a social system modernizes, informal means of resolving private disputes break down (McIntosh, 1983). This breakdown creates a greater collective dependence on the judicial system. Courts reach a certain capacity, or "litigation threshold," and litigation levels off. Alternatively, the leveling off comes as a result of the redevelopment of relationships destroyed in the initial surge toward modernity. These relationships become a basis for informal social control and the resolution of conflict.

McIntosh's (1983) study of the rate of civil litigation in a trial court from 1820 to 1977 shows that court capacity puts a limit on formal disputing. In addition, there seem to be cyclical patterns of litigation depending on the socioeconomic conditions of the jurisdiction. Of note is the finding that litigation may take on the characteristics of political action, and the conflict of goals and values normally fought in political arenas finds its ways into the courts.

Engel's study of a small Illinois county indicates that although contract actions were almost ten times as frequent as personal injury cases, it was the latter that created the greatest amount of reaction in the community (Engel, 1984). The negative attitude toward litigation derives from the belief that people should settle their own differences—a surprising conclusion given the parallel concern in contemporary society about too much self-help and too little reported crime.

As Galanter (1983) points out, our use of litigation is not surprising given the changes in technology, the knowledge base available for solving disputes, and the greater access to courts. However, overshadowing the change in disputing patterns are changes in the symbolic aspects of the system. There is more law than before. Our experience of most of it is increasingly indirect and mediated. Most disputing leads to mediation or bargaining, rather than authoritative disposition by the courts. However, the courts occupy a significant part of the **symbolic** universe and litigation seems omnipresent (Galanter, 1983:70).

Galanter (1983) argues that the view of litigation as a destructive force, undermining other social institutions, is misleadingly one-sided.

If litigation marks the assertion of individual will, it is also a reaching out for communal help and affirmation. If some litigation challenges accepted practice, it is an instrument for testing the quality of present consensus. It provides a forum for moving issues from the realm of unilateral power into a realm of public accountability. By permitting older clusters of practice to be challenged and new ones tested and incorporated into the constellation it helps to "create a new paradigm for the establishment of stable community life." (Galanter, 1983:70)

The reactive nature of the courts is seen in their handling of disputes by putting the emphasis on the use of alternatives when they are unable to deal with all the problems that people encounter.

Galanter (1983:35) argues that not only has there been a shift in the pattern of cases coming into the courts but there have also been changes in what has taken place when these cases are filed. First, it appears that in the United States, in federal appeals courts, state supreme courts, and civil courts, most cases tend to be disposed off without a full adversary trial. Voluntary dismissal, possibly as a result of settlement, and uncontested judgment are the most commonly recorded event in these courts. Studies suggest that although litigation rates have risen, the per capita rates of contested cases have declined. In the same fashion, there has been a decline in the per capita rate of cases eliciting written opinions from the state supreme courts (Galanter, 1983:44).

There have been other changes in the character of what courts do. Less of their work is directed toward decisive resolution of individual disputes and more is involved in routine administration and supervised bargaining. As pointed out by Pruet and Glick, courtroom behavior tends to be cooperative rather than conflictual, bureaucratic rather than adversarial. "Judges, prosecutors, and defense lawyers often share many common goals and concerns, and in order to achieve these goals they strive for cooperation and consensus" (Pruet & Glick, 1986:9). Courts, Galanter (1983) maintains, contribute to the settlement of disputes less by imposing authoritative resolutions and more by setting patterns and by mediating. When litigation does take place it is more exacting and more time consuming, perhaps reflecting the complexity of cases that are not resolvable through informal means.

Further, courts have shifted over time to dealing more with criminal than civil cases. Galanter (1983:42) points out that over the past century in the United States there has been a pronounced shift in the character of the cases brought to regular trial courts. An increasing number of criminal relative to civil cases has been brought to the attention of the courts. On the civil side, there has been a shift from cases involving market transactions (contract, property, and debt collection) to family and tort cases.

The movement toward more involvement in criminal cases, in particular, may reflect the courts' concern for careful attention to due process in these instances, discouraging the move toward informal treatment (a point made previously). This view has come under attack from two sides. On the one hand, the focus on due process may be seen as a lever for the accused to manipulate the system in his or her favor to escape punishment. On the other hand, it may be criticized as ignoring the benefits of community-based programs that handle minor crime in informal ways, thus avoiding a costly trial and the stigma of criminalization. This process leaves unresolved the basis for the conflict that led to the crime. For example, in Canadian courts juveniles are separated from an understanding of the action taken against them, which leaves them unable to take account of the conflict that the court process has imposed on them. Following the arguments of Christie (1977), presented in Chapter 5, Hackler and Garapon (1986) state that the welfare-oriented juvenile court of the past few decades may have stolen conflicts and humiliated families with resolutions imposed by social workers. The goal was to convert cases of conflict to nonconflict, as the goal of the earlier Juvenile Delinquent Act was to heal the sick. However, while juveniles are being analyzed by professionals, they are given no opportunity to express their problems, acquiescing to a conflict resolution by those used to handling it. The new Canadian Young Offenders Act, Hackler and Garapon argue, has done little to improve this situation. The difficulties for juveniles in making sense of the criminal courts and their interpretations of their conflicts are equally applicable to other groups in society.

The Role of Key Actors in Court

The police play an important role in bringing disputes to court. Galanter (1983:26) points out that the police may make an arrest or file charges for purposes of control with no intention of pursuing prosecution. Katz (1979:443) says that the police also frequently make arrests in response to situational pressures, for example, to break up a domestic dispute or barroom fight, with little or no thought to later stages of the criminal enforcement process.

> Even when agents specifically set out to construct cases that can be prosecuted, they frequently make ill considered arrests under emergency conditions. A drug sale may be "going down" in an apartment that contains numerous people with varying degrees of involvement in the transaction...if someone identifies an undercover agent inside or detects surveillance outside and "all hell breaks loose," everyone who can be fitted into the agents' cars may be arrested. (Katz, 1979:443)

What this means, according to Katz, is that by the time the case reaches the prosecutor, no one in the criminal justice system may want to devote further time and resources to pursuing it. Prosecutors, he says, frequently find cases to be less serious than the initial charges, which may have been invoked under time pressure or justified by emergency measures. The process of arrest may be seen as sufficient punishment under these conditions.

Other key actors in the dispute process are the lawyers, who are important in transforming disputes. As Galanter (1983:19) points out, lawyers help translate clients' disputes to fit into acceptable legal categories. But lawyers may also act as gatekeepers, screening out those cases they are not inclined to pursue.

Feeley (1979) argues that as reliance on professionalism and improved technology has increased, the role of the amateur in the criminal process, in particular, has decreased. An illustration is provided by the negative experience of a group in Toronto called the Church of the Universe. Through its "Universe University" a course in legal self-defense is provided for lay members to defend themselves on charges of possession of their sacrament, marijuana. This group has had some success in the courts. However, as one crown attorney points out, self-appointed lawyers exasperate judges. They don't know how to play by the rules and have an "excruciatingly low" success rate. Almost all who lose lose needlessly to technical inadequacies in their cases regardless of their guilt or innocence (*Globe and Mail* 1984b:A9).

As the law expanded its protection of liberty (of contract) and (corporate) property, it relentlessly stifled alternatives (Auerbach, 1983:140). A paradox appears, according to Auerbach: The more elaborate and sophisticated our legal culture, the more serious is the problem of access to justice. Campbell and Talarico (1983) found in a survey of respondents in three Georgia cities that a two-stage process is involved in acquiring legal services (even when there is no cost to the user). The first stage involves individuals' views of whether or not they need a lawyer to handle their problems. At this stage, a distinct racial and socioeconomic difference appears in respondents' views. Blacks, the poor, and those with little education are least likely to think they needed a lawyer in the previous two years. Campbell and Talarico speculate that this disinclination to use legal services comes from a widespread disenchantment by these groups with the justice system.

Second, it seems likely that these groups also do not use lawyers because they feel lawyers are irrelevant to the process of solving life's problems. Instead, they are more inclined to invoke self-help mechanisms to bring about resolution. Third, it may be that these groups are simply less well informed about legal services and benefits lawyers can offer individuals involved in legal problems.

At the second stage of hiring a lawyer, actually making contact when a need for a lawyer has been established, there is no difference in response across groups.

This refinement of access to lawyers highlights the point made by Auerbach that law is always more than rules and procedures, statutes and precedents, or courts and lawyers. "It is, ultimately, an ideology, a set of beliefs and a system of integrated values that provide elements of predictability, stability, and coherence" (Auerbach, 1983:142). The difficult task that lawyers have in promoting this ideal is to develop legitimacy for all users, not just those who are seen to be advantaged by their privileged position in society. The sense of legitimacy must promote law that not only is just but also is not seen as unjust.

In a similar fashion, the participation of judges in active promotion of settlements in court cases is happening more often and is more respectable (Galanter, 1983:23). The major reason given for this activity is that a movement away from a strict model of adjudication is necessary to relieve overburdensome case loads. But, further, judges get involved because the litigants want it. This involvement is requested as much to repair relations between disputants as to get a decision. Participation by judges is often a reflection of community standards. There appears to be a close relationship between what the community finds acceptable in resolving disputes and what the court (especially the civil court) adjudicates (Engel, 1983).

Even with extensive screening of cases, courts are overwhelmed and looked for alternatives, raising a question about judicial overwork and capacity. Alternatives that have been tried to reduce this overwork include a program developed in Riverside, California, Superior Court, where a judge has been assigned specifically to handle settlement conferences in civil cases. As Rich explains, "in just ten months the settlement conference procedure (mediation) resulted in the complete elimination of the chronic backlog. The civil active list was completely wiped out" (Rich, 1980:530).

The drop in court congestion and the satisfaction of the users seem to offer this as a truly viable option to civil court procedures. Its application to criminal cases would seem to lie in the discretion the judge is given in using alternative means in resolving diputes when there has been a breach of criminal law, especially those in which there have been personal assault and injury. The demand for adjudicative treatment of criminal cases in a desire for punishment makes the search for alternatives more difficult. The willingness of the judiciary to accept these approaches may motivate the policy makers to look at them more closely.

Attorneys and their clients settle numerous other lawsuits among themselves after the scheduling of a settlement conference but before the conference date. Litigants, Rich (1980) claims, overwhelmingly prefer the settlement method as it is inexpensive, quicker (one to two hours versus two weeks for a trial), more manageable in terms of outcome, and less anxiety provoking. In addition, the litigants avoid having a settlement imposed on them but can instead search for a solution that satisfies both sides. Rich, a Superior Court Judge working with this system in California, argues for mediation over adjudication. Lack of training in mediation can be overcome by educating judges to deal with problems in this fashion.

Burger (1982:275) advocates training in negotiation for others in the legal profession. He says that of all the skills needed for a practicing lawyer, skill in negotiation must rank very high. This call for training has resulted in some innovations in law school curricula (see, e.g., Sander, 1984).[2]

How does the legal profession respond to these options? Lawyers are generally responsive to alternatives, although sensitive to the loss of revenue they may generate. In a description of the success of the divorce mediation program offered in the state of Maine, the director of Court Mediation Services was quoted as saying that he had received a large number of requests for information from around the country and around the world. The most commonly asked question was "What effect does it have on lawyers' fees? Does it hurt their pocketbooks?" He was able to assure them that it has had no perceptible effect on their income (*Biddeford Journal Tribune*, 1986a).

Access to Justice

McEwan and Maiman argue that the most important costs of rules and procedures that deny the poor and weak access to adjudication may be that the disadvantaged are also effectively denied the opportunity to settle claims informally. "Without the expansion of legal rights and resources for disadvantaged parties [they lose] their ability to impose costs and risks and thus to bargain effectively" (McEwan & Maiman, 1984:46). In many instances, formal justice is more accessible than mediation or arbitration, but to inexperienced litigants, this process is harder to manage and more difficult to halt when it is in their interest to do so.

Alternatives to courts have sprung up, McEwan and Maiman say, as part of an access-to-negotiation movement. These options appear in small claims courts, where lawyers (acting as professional negotiators) are often absent. They have appeared in divorce courts, where emotions run high, preventing attorneys from examining options through negotiations. They have appeared in criminal courts, where the state has taken the place of the victim, precluding any negotiation between the original parties.

---

[2] The Sander piece is one of a number of curricula-related articles presented in the issue on Alternative Dispute Resolution in the Law Curriculum, *Journal of Legal Education*.

In these and similar settings, inexperienced court users may find themselves caught in a process they cannot predict or control. Court-sponsored mediation or negotiation can be viewed as a mechanism for reestablishing control by the disputant over both the conflict and its resolution in the context of a new bargaining relationship defined by the potential for an adjudicated settlement. (McEwan & Maiman, 1984:47)

Vidmar (1985) characterizes this distinction between mediation and adjudication as revolving around consent versus coercion. In mediation the parties have decisional power, whereas in adjudication the third party (e.g., the judge) has decisional power. Vidmar maintains that cases in which defendants deny all liability are more likely to be adjudicated. Those cases in which there is an admission of partial or full liability are more likely to be settled by mediation. This experience in the small claims courts may have important parallels in the criminal courts, as well, where admission of guilt allows for negotiation of sentence and denial leads to full adjudication.

FORMAL RULES AND INFORMAL PRACTICES IN THE COURTS

Negotiating Guilt through Plea Bargaining

As we have seen, the law as administered by the police is often negotiated through discretion concerning arrest. The same is true in the courts, where the discretion to prosecute or to adjust sentencing through bargaining with offenders changes the view of courts as strictly forums for upholding conformity to law. Plea bargaining, a common practice in North American courts, is a form of exchange. The criminal is normally brought before the court on the initiative of the state, represented by the prosecution. "In criminal cases the function of settling conflicts receded at the expense of the task of upholding conformity with the laws" (Aubert, 1967:41).

Sarat and Grossman point out that plea bargaining is less like other forms of adjudication, in which the role of judge and adversary are clearly separated, and more like the kind of dyadic negotiations that precede resort to adjudication. The defendant is seen to be in "conflict with the law" and is induced to settle through an informal bargaining process. Rather than the judge, the public prosecutor takes on the role of "dispute settler" and has a great deal of discretion concerning whether to prosecute or on what charge. "He has available both the coercive power of the state (in the form of a probable guilty verdict if the case goes to trial) and the discretion to work out an acceptable compromise" (Sarat & Grossman, 1975:1205).

Mediating toward a compromise is in the prosecutors' interests because it allows them to reduce their case load and better control the outcome of cases. "In place of the formality of court adjudication of guilt or innocence, the prosecutor becomes the manager of a ritualized conflict resolution ceremony" (Sarat & Grossman, 1975:1205). Galanter (1983:27) claims that these nontrial dispositions account for about 80 or 90 percent more of criminal dispositions in almost every American jurisdiction. In these cases, the judges may be passive, agreeing to the deal that is struck by the parties. Most often, however, the judge takes an active role in the plea-bargaining process. Ryan and Alfini (1979) argue that judges' role in the plea-bargaining process is constrained by their view of their own skills at negotiation and the structure of the courts in which they operate. They conclude, however, that most judges are involved in the negotiation process.

Galanter (1983:28) says that judges justify active participation in plea bargaining on the grounds that such efforts provide greater satisfaction to litigants, repair relations between contesting parties, and avoid untoward results in particular cases. This presents a picture of the courts as being more willing to come to terms with the reality of social conflict needing flexible solutions than with the demand for application of law in a rigid and unbending fashion. This acknowledges the need for sustaining social relationships and removing litigants from adversarial positions which require an adjudicative decision about winners and losers.

In a critique of plea bargaining, Alschuler (1979) argues that this form of court-supported negotiation consists of an exchange of official concessions for the act of self-conviction. The concessions that the defendant receives may relate to sentence, the offense charged, or other circumstances of the case. The benefit offered by the defendant is always the same—entry of a plea of guilty (Alschuler, 1979:213). This denies the defendant due process, trading off constitutional rights for more lenient treatment.

Schulhofer (1984) claims that plea bargaining is not inevitable. Rather, judges and lawyers have "chosen" to process cases in that way. "We can cease imposing a price, in months or years of incarceration, upon defendants who exercise that privilege, and can instead permit or even encourage defendants to ask for a hearing in which they may put the prosecution to its proof" (Schulhofer, 1984:1107). Schulhofer demands that cases not reflect "intuitive or off-the-cuff compromise" but the considered application of law to facts proved in open court.

In response to these criticisms, Church (1979) reasons that a system that confers sentence discounts on those defendants who waive their adversarial determination of guilt need not violate either the tenets of rationality in the penal law or the constitution. "Negotiated dispositions in a properly constructed system will approximate the probable results of trial, and any remaining distance between the bargained disposition and 'what would have been' the result of the trial involves no inherent illegitimacy" (Church, 1979:512). Provided the defendant is apprised of his or her rights, and has access to an attorney throughout the process, Church feels that the plea bargain can provide flexibility that does not exist in the formal application of the law.

A separate critique of the plea-bargaining process is directed toward the leniency that it offers to offenders who should be treated more punitively but who opt, instead, for lesser punishment. Plea bargaining is often seen as an administrative expediency, especially in overworked urban jurisdictions (Church, 1979:510). The resulting sentences suffer from a lack of justification by any rationale for penal sanction, whether deterrence, societal protection, rehabilitation, or whatever. "When this argument is combined with the preceding due process critique, the current system is placed in the unenviable position of being assaulted by civil libertarians and law-and-order advocates at the same time" (Church, 1979:510).

Public Opinion and Plea Bargaining

The strategy used in plea bargaining seems dependent on the public awareness and attitude toward the major crimes being pursued. The pressure of public opinion reduces the likelihood that prosecutors will plea bargain on more serious crimes (Hartnagel, 1975:47). According to Pritchard, prosecution is a political process and prosecutors have a stake in how their actions are perceived. Maintaining a public image of a crime fighter is important. This need may translate into pressing for trial, regardless of the strength of the evidence against a defendant. Pritchard reports strong effects of the media coverage of offenses as setting the agenda for prosecutorial handling of plea negotiation in major crimes. He says that the amount of space newspapers were willing to devote to the typical story about a case was a stronger predictor than any other variable in his study of whether or not the prosecutor would negotiate (Pritchard, 1986:155).

Obviously, in less notorious cases, plea bargaining continues because of its effectiveness in processing cases in criminal courts. In its defense, as well, Church points out that a conscientious prosecutor, mindful of his or her responsibility to protect the public welfare, might rationally conclude that the certainty of a lower sentence may be preferable to the risk of acquittal at trial. The defendant exchanges the chance of complete exoneration for the security of a judgment less onerous than that which might be imposed after trial. "Each party thus trades the possibility of total victory for the certainty of avoiding total defeat" (Church, 1979:518).

Restricting Plea Bargaining
through Mandatory Sentencing

An alternative to plea bargaining is mandatory sentencing, which should restrict the discretion of the prosecutor and the judge in their decisions about charging and sentencing. In fact, in their study of the enactment of mandatory charging and sentencing introduced to curtail gun use in criminal actions in Wayne County, Michigan, Heumann and Loftin (1979) argue that mandatory sentences do reduce judicial discretion but are accompanied by an increase in prosecutorial discretion. Plea-bargaining restrictions, on the other hand, reduce prosecutorial discretion but lead to an increase in judicial discretion.

What happens if both forms of discretion are restricted at the same time? Heumann and Loftin report that even with the commitment by the Wayne County prosecutor to have all his subordinates fall into line in the implementation of the mandatory charging, other mechanisms came into play, providing functional equivalents of prosecutorial plea bargaining. "In serious cases (armed robberies, some of the assaults) sentence bargaining and sentence adjustments allowed defendants to plead with as much assurance of the outcome as they would have before the innovations— and sometimes with more" (Heumann & Loftin, 1979:425). The judges adjusted sentencing downward to include the mandatory two-year period for breach of the gun law, thus reflecting previous sentencing patterns for serious crimes.

Heumann and Loftin conclude that rigid policies of mandatory sentencing and proscriptions on plea bargaining force criminal court actors to make adjustments that are unstructured, ad hoc, sometimes contrary to the law, and sometimes unsuccessful (Heumann & Loftin, 1979:427). In this case, the need for discretion comes from the demands of the system to be flexible in handling the conflict that comes into it. This need is reflected in the widespread use and persistence of plea bargaining.

Plea Bargaining: Coercion or Compromise?

Despite its extensive use in many jurisdictions (Canada, see Hartnagel, 1975; Britain, see Baldwin & McConville, 1977; United States, see Buckle & Buckle, 1977), there are still serious criticisms directed against the coercive aspects of plea bargaining, in which individuals may be blackmailed into pleading guilty to achieve a conviction (Baldwin & McConville, 1977). Its historical precedents are questioned, as well. Alschuler points out that there is no historical evidence that plea bargaining has always been with us, especially since guilty pleas were discouraged in early courtrooms prior to trial, partly because of the severity of sentencing imposed on the individual in capital cases (Alschuler, 1979). Despite these arguments, the persistence of plea bargaining makes us wonder if its justification comes only from its efficiency[3] since the courtroom actors ignore its detrimental effects on the guarantees of due process.

Smith (1986), in reviewing cases from courts in a number of American cities, found that there was no evidence that plea bargaining is coercive. It is claimed that plea bargaining makes possible a dual sentencing structure in which defendants who proceed to trial are sentenced more harshly than those who plead guilty. The data Smith has examined indicates that when actual sentences are compared against expected sentences, there is little support for the coercion argument.

Maynard argues, further, that plea bargaining is not a "response" to such outside factors as overcrowding in the courts or harsh penalties established by state legislatures. Rather, plea bargaining is an "enactment" of participants' discourse and negotiation skills in managing conflict in courtrooms. Their enactment reflects the negotiator's associations with defendants and witnesses, involvement in their own offices and professions, connections with other agencies (e.g., police and schools), and contact with the court and its own activities (e.g., trial). "We can thus speak of negotiating procedures as being sensitive to an array of social networks within and surrounding bargaining encounters" (Maynard, 1984:208).

This view does not argue for the inevitability of plea bargaining. It does help explain its place in the court as a social environment, where attempts are made to make sense of the conflict brought to it through a negotiation of guilt or innocence. This mediative process embodied in the plea-bargaining process recognizes the conflicting demands of the public, the judge, the prosecutor, the defendant, and the victim. If further underlines the continuing attempt to set boundaries of crime by invoking formal and informal mechanisms for inclusion or exclusion of certain acts from this definition.

The Limits of Judicial Discretion

It should be clear in this discussion that the court handles only a few of the cases that pass through the filter of public nonreporting, police screening, and prosecutor discretion. Galanter (1983) outlines ten different types of cases that survive the review process of informal procedures and settlement in courts and end up being fully adjudicated.

1. Cases are adjudicated when there is a need for judicial declaration, as in divorce or probate (a presettlement may have occurred but ratification is still necessary).

---

[3] Schulhofer (1988) argues strenuously that, in fact, plea bargaining is economically inefficient.

2. Cut-and-dried cases such as collection cases are adjudicated when the defendant frequently does not appear and there is little contest.
3. Adjudication takes place because the prosecutor feels unable to drop or reduce the charges, especially when there is great notoriety.
4. An individual may pursue a case to prove that he or she has gone the limit in getting recompense.
5. Cases are adjudicated when the complexity of the issues may make settlement too unwieldy or costly.
6. Settlement may provide insufficient value and adjudication becomes the best choice; for example, criminals facing mandatory sentences may opt for adjudication rather then settle.
7. Litigants may feel that the bargaining process will reduce their credibility for future negotiations.
8. A party may want to adjudicate to affect the state of the law, especially to protect the litigant's position in any future controversies.
9. Parties may pursue adjudication for vindication of fundamental value commitments, such as demonstrated in church-state litigation.
10. Governments may pursue decisions to establish public policy standards for settlement.

SUMMARY

The fact that we have dealt poorly with resolving conflict-based crime in the past need not preclude us from investigating these alternatives more carefully in the future. Hagan, Hewitt, and Alwin (1979) argue that this process of administering conflict through the different roles that various actors play in the courtroom can lead to the "loose coupling" of component parts of the criminal justice system, which affect the nature of the treatment individuals receive. They argue that the role of probation officials seems highly ritualistic, whereas the prosecutors are more highly integrated with the judiciary in sentencing. What this means for conflict resolution is that the individualistic information brought into court to assist in the deliberations is not easily incorporated into the trial process, mainly because it often impedes the efficient operation of the judicial organization. That the organizational structure of the courts can play such an important role in the processing of criminal complaints points to the possibility that the conflict that is the basis for the complaints is not adequately addressed.

The problems with courts, according to Cavanagh and Sarat (1980:377), are a result of change in both private and public institutions and in social practices. "As authority in families, churches, and schools has eroded, and as new burdens have been placed on government bodies other than courts, the courts have been asked to cope with problems that have sapped the strength of alternative institutions" (Cavanagh & Sarat, 1980:376).

Courts are often an inappropriate forum for some of the disputes that are brought to them, encouraging the legal profession to search for ways of diverting some of the work that comes their way. A related problem derives from the inconclusiveness of judgments, which may lead to disenchantment with the legal system and further problems of conflict.

In coming to grips with the role that courts have in developing more flexible responses to community conflict, we have to assess them as forums for negotiating social order versus arenas for delivering punishment and enhancing deterrence. The extensive use of informal tactics in screening and managing cases show the courts to be utilizing negotiation and mediation as informal mechanisms for setting boundaries for designating what is and is not criminal. In addition, the courts use bargaining in those cases identified as criminal to offer an accommodation to the constraints of the courts and the demands of the defendants. In identifying these areas of discretion we have outlined new ideas for the examination of the inevitability of negotiating what is and is not criminal. In the future we must provide a clearer evaluation of what occurs in plea bargaining and what alternatives exist to diversion and probation; and we must outline the role that mandatory sentencing and charging play in affecting this mediative role of the courts.

CHAPTER 8

Summary of Propositions and Research Agenda for Conflict-based Criminology

INTRODUCTION

In laying out the arguments related to the treatment programs for offenders, Martinson points out that they are based on a theory of crime as a disease—something foreign and abnormal that can be cured. This theory may be flawed because it overlooks, and in fact denies, both the normality of crime in society and the normality of the response of offenders to the facts and conditions of our society (Martinson, 1974:49). This perspective sees crime as a "social phenomenon," suggesting that prevention, through deterrence, may be a more effective "treatment" for crime than the rehabilitative strategies offered for those who have already offended.

As pointed out earlier, two separate models of law that have existed side by side in the People's Republic of China illustrate the conceptualization of crime deterrence and crime as social phenomenon. Both conflict and crime are dealt with through routinized means of conflict resolution. The two models of crime are differentiated as "external" and "internal."

The external model rests on formal, usually written rules; a rationalized system of government; and specialists in administration (Johnson, 1986). The internal model tries to achieve compliance through a lengthy educational process, in which individuals learn and internalize socially acceptable values and norms. 'When individuals fail to conform through self-control, spontaneous social pressure arises to correct the deviants" (Johnson, 1986:452). As Johnson points out, this internal model promotes the Chinese preference for extralegal mediation of disputes over formal adjudication. The internal model is implemented within a control system that does not observe the traditional Western demarcation of boundaries between government and private spheres of social organization (Johnson, 1986:452). An important aspect of this control relates to the deescalation of conflict.

The Chinese view of the coexistence of two forms of justice helps highlight what we in North America have treated as an implicit aspect of social control. The cultural differences between these societies preclude an assumption of the direct applicability of these models to our society. However, the clear message in this comparison is the fact, as discussed in the previous chapters, that we cannot understand the workings of the formal system of social control without a clear understanding of the complementary workings of the informal system. Our response to crime actually reflects these complementary models. The preceding text has sought to articulate how they operate in affecting our definitions of the origins and evolution of conflict and crime. We will conclude this discussion with a series of propositions that summarize these relationships and outline areas for future research.

PROPOSITIONS FOR THE STUDY OF CONFLICT-BASED CRIMINOLOGY

1. Conflict and crime are related through the ever-changing boundaries that conflict draws around crime. To understand the origins of much crime, we must first understand conflict.

Crime is set in a sea of conflict. Defining the borders of crime depends on the extent to which we accept the breach of law and our tolerance for conflict requiring legal versus extralegal (community-based) responses. Public acceptance of the normalcy of crime is reflected in the extent of nonreporting of crime. Failure to report misbehavior to police is due in part to fear, but it may arise, as well, from a belief that disagreements have been resolved.

Conflict brings out the need for the application of rules that, had no conflict occurred, might have remained dormant and forgotten. It is the development and enforcement of these rules that define the borders between conflict and crime.

2. Conflict in society is inevitable. The inevitability of crime is tempered by the application of legal definitions to its management and the capacity of social organizations to reduce its escalation.

Changing from law to custom does not suggest that deviant behavior will be eliminated but only that it will no longer be illegal (Hilbert & Wright, 1982). Conflict remains in society and forms the base for interpersonal disputes, whether defined as criminal or not. The struggle for power or the attempt to provide socialization to societal norms clearly helps explain different aspects of this dispute-based process. Social conflict is inevitable, with crime as a less predictable outgrowth of the legal interpretations of the consequences of personal disputes.

3. The prevention of crime includes a need to deescalate or, at least, contain conflict.

There is no strong empirical support for the view that groups promoting deviant subcultures also promote violence, when violence is considered an integral aspect of the group's functioning (Hagan, 1985). Instead, there are no norms in these groups to deescalate violence once it begins. The emphasis, then, is less on the promotion of conflict and more on its control, a shift from a subcultural explanation to one based on socialization (or social control theory).

4. We often treat crime in mediative ways but define it in nonnegotiable terms. A change in perspective to reflect the former over the latter would emphasize mediation and negotiation over treatment and cure.

Definitions of crime through law may be seen as immutable. Law, after all, determines guilt or innocence. This rule can vary, however, depending on circumstances, public tolerance, and judicial discretion. The criminal justice system uses the law not only to deter crime and punish criminals but also to reduce social disorder, which may be threatening or dangerous. Any study of crime needs to account for behavior that has these characteristics but is not yet unlawful because it has not come to the attention of the police or they have chosen to ignore it.

Community-based mediation, among other alternatives, has been offered as a way of dealing with these problems of disorder. Alternative, or informal, responses have to be accounted for in any definition of crime, even though they do not have any specific legal sanction. They create the outside limits of criminality by complementing the criminal justice response to misbehavior.

5. The role of third-party individuals in escalating or deescalating disputes can play an important part in our response to this conflict. The informal response leaves the dispute as conflict whereas the formal response criminalizes it, reducing the chance of negotiation taking place instead of punishment.

Factors that help explain the outcome and consequences of the expansion of a dispute include the degree of dissatisfaction (both in intensity and scope) with the established order in society; the extent to which those who are unhappy with the established order for reasons of their own would benefit from an ordering of issues along the lines suggested in the expansion; the timing of the emergence of a particular case in relation to other, similar ones; the particular constellation of facts and issues on the case itself; the relation of redefinition to parallel political cleavages; and the extent to which an audience becomes involved in the disputing process, giving credibility and support to the shift in perspective in the dispute (Mather & Yngvesson, 1980–81:798).

6. The discretion used in criminalizing conflict is affected by relationships between the disputants and/or attitudes toward the police.

Despite the illegality of selective enforcement and the power it puts into the hands of police officers, the overreach of the law requires the selective enforcement of laws in policing (Klockars, 1985). The tension between law and order is complex because there is often ambiguity in the application of the rule of law (Skolnick, 1966). Varying definitions are based on community-based standards of what is acceptable behavior under the law. The police may be given discretion in their handling of conflict in the community. The discretion may lead, however, to a lessening of legal sanction in exchange for order.

The police are more reactive than proactive in situations in which they are asked for assistance or there is a clearly defined victim. Further, in cases of social conflict in which the antagonists are intimate or there is some sense that the parties are able to take care of their own problems, the police may simply ignore the situation, keeping disputants from entering the criminal justice system even though they prefer to use this alternative. Police, then, can arrest, remove one party from the scene, attempt to settle the argument, or simply do nothing at all (Smith & Klein, 1984:468).

7. The criminalizing of disputes transforms them into adversarial action for treatment by lawyers and judges. This process renders them difficult to mediate by the parties themselves.

There are, in fact, too few conflicts in society (Christie, 1977), partly because they are taken over by lawyers and the criminal justice professionals. These conflicts in the hands of professionals become nonconflicts. They are handed back to the disputants as resolved when often they do not meet the disputants' needs. There is little chance for the individuals themselves to participate in the resolution of the conflict. Bureaucratic solutions, for better or worse, are provided to the disputants (Aubert, 1967). This system may assure due process and equitable outcomes, but it also restricts individuals from participating in the different stages of their conflict, ensuring a solution that fits their own circumstances.

8. Deterring crime requires the application of informal sanction to complement the threat of formal action.

If persons believe that others will disapprove of their arrest for committing a certain act, and they refrain from that activity because they fear the stigma of getting caught, this constitutes general deterrence, with a legal sanction as the source (Williams & Hawkins, 1986). It could be said, as well, that if the risk of arrest is perceived as low, with minimal chance of severe punishment, deterrence would occur through the stigma attached to being involved in the crime itself. The fear of stigma stems from the act, not the sanction, and thus is extralegal (Williams & Hawkins, 1986:563). Our fixation on formal response has led us to believe that the system needs to become more punitive in order to deter crime. In fact, the justice system has usurped too much of the deterrence role and left informal systems of control without the ability to provide this sanction. The difference in the perception of severity may be a difference in the perception of the loss of the social bond that occurs with the exacted punishment. Punishment deters, but this punishment need not be legal. It can be just as effective if it results from a withdrawal of affection or the weakening of social bonds.

9. The demand for alternative forms of justice has been created by an overloading of formal justice systems. This result highlights the need to institutionalize complementary systems of informal social control.

Courts have become overworked because North Americans are increasingly turning to formal justice for relief from a range of personal distresses and anxieties. "The courts have been expected to fill the void created by the decline of church, family, and neighborhood unity" (Burger, 1982:275). Alternative justice is offered not only to unclog the courts but also to offer more humane alternatives to litigation.

10. The escalation of conflict to crime reflects a desire on the part of the disputants for punishment of one another.

Citizens often do not use alternatives voluntarily because by the time a conflict is serious enough to justify bringing in a third party, the disputants do not want what alternatives have to offer as a solution. "At this point, the grievant wants vindication, protection of his or her rights (as he or she perceives them), an advocate to help in the battle, and a third party to uncover the 'truth' and declare the other party wrong" (Merry & Silbey, 1984:152). Before the escalation of the dispute, courts are the location of last resort as most disputants prefer to handle the problem by themselves.

11. Formal justice processes use discretion extensively to respond to crime, either through mediation or plea bargaining. This use requires a recognition of the negotiated aspects of crime and conflict management in courts and court-annexed programs.

Definitions of crime depend on our beliefs about human nature and the effectiveness of the criminal justice system. The negotiation of justice is a reflection not only of what the agents of social control **can do** but also what they are **prepared to do** in attacking crime.

12. The extent of crime is affected by the degree to which individuals negotiate their own settlements of the conflict they encounter, either through self-help or avoidance, rather than drawing it to the attention of the police or the courts.

Deterrence provided by knowledge of possible retribution, or self-help, is of a different kind than that supported by formal law. The use of crime to deter crime is more widespread and effective than is commonly accepted by criminologists, as it is not precluded by the justice system's capacity (Pontell, 1978). Further, the courts favor leniency in responding to crimes committed as self-help.

CONFLICT, CRIME, AND CONFLICT MANAGEMENT

The description of the prevalence of conflict-based crime makes us aware of the ever-changing nature of legal definitions and social responses to misbehavior. What should be evident, as well, is that this view of crime need not preclude the insights provided by already established criminological perspectives, such as social control or subcultural theories. It allows for a broadening of the scope of these sociological frameworks to include noncrime as well as crime in the explanation of criminality. The role that social institutions play in directing our behavior both through positive rewards and through informal deterrence must be included in any equation that explains the factors that are to be included in reducing criminality. If crime is conflict based, and much of it seems to be, its prevention rests on the reduction of this conflict.

The criticism that we are not addressing pathological crime or that we cannot realistically deal with property crime has already been examined. What should not be ignored in the study of crime is that it is not a social phenomenon containing homogeneous parts. There are many different types of crime, and it would be foolish to suggest one explanation for all of it. The conceptual basis for the approach here is that in recognizing the different types of crime, we recognize the different social factors that define them as criminal, lead to their emergence from other social behavior, respond to their enactment, seek to restrict and contain them, and punish those who commit them.

This conflict-based perspective allows us, as well, to take account of the role that the victim plays in the criminal event. Criminal justice agencies are beginning to recognize the rights of victims. What is apparent is that many crimes do not reach formal agencies because victims fail to report them. It is clear that nonreporting reduces the formal sanction applied to misbehavior, but it may reflect, as well, the role that informal negotiation plays in bringing about resolution of conflict-based crime in the community. This resolution need not take the form of vigilantism or fearful withdrawal but can be seen to contain an element of self-regulation in the negotiation of a peaceful settlement between conflicting parties.

It is often the case, however, that individuals need help to find this solution. The formal response is to punish, or threaten to punish, the offender. The informal response includes the idea of teaching people that violence is bad and will be negatively sanctioned by family, friends, and employers. The reduction of violence, then, requires the combined efforts of the police and the community.

This conflict-based perspective on crime should broaden our view of the successes or failures in the administration of justice and the role that the police and courts can play in working with the community to reduce crime.

We can pursue these questions through a concerted research effort, which not only examines national trends in crime generation but also raises questions about what can be learned from cross-national research. We have used examples in this book from China, Canada, Great Britain, and the United States. These societies differ not only in their crime rates but also in their tolerance of conflict. More work needs to be done to examine how conflict-based crime differs in varied circumstances and to determine where the successes and failures have been experienced in dealing with this problem. This study can range from the examination of family violence to research on homicide. The war on crime can be supplemented by lessons learned in conflict management. Future research is needed, then, to examine the social roots of criminality and the complementary efforts of community and criminal justice agencies to define the borders of crime.

References

Abel, Richard L. 1982. "The Contradictions of Informal Justice." In Richard L. Abel (ed.), *The Politics of Informal Justice:* Vol. 1, *The American Experience,* pp. 267–320. New York: Academic Press.

Adler, Peter. 1987. "Is ADR a Social Movement?" *Negotiation Journal,* 3 (1):59–71.

Akers, Ronald L. 1977. *Deviant Behavior: A Social Learning Approach.* Belmont, Calif.: Wadsworth.

Alderson, J. 1985. "Police and Public Order." *Public Administration,* 63 (4):435–444.

Alschuler, Albert W. 1979. "Plea Bargaining and Its History." *Law and Society Review,* 13 (2):212–245.

American Arbitration Association. 1982. Community Dispute Services. Unpublished manuscript, San Francisco.

American Bar Association. 1985. Mediation in the Schools. Washington, D.C.: Special Committee on Dispute Resolution.

———. 1986. Dispute Resolution Program Directory 1986–87. Washington, D.C.: Special Committee on Dispute Resolution.

Aubert, Vilhelm. 1967. "Courts and Conflict Resolution." *Journal of Conflict Resolution,* XI (1):40–51.

Auerbach, Jerold S. 1983. *Justice Without Law?* New York: Oxford University Press.

Baldwin, John, & Michael McConville. 1977. *Negotiated Justice: Pressures to Plead Guilty.* London: Martin Robertson.

Bard, Morton, & Joseph Zacker. 1976. "How Police Handle Explosive Squabbles." *Psychology Today,* 10 (Nov.):71ff.

Beer, Jennifer E. 1986. *Peacemaking in Your Neighborhood: Reflections on an*

Experiment in Community Mediation. Philadelphia: Friends Suburban Project.

Beresford, Robert, & Jill Cooper, 1977. "A Neighborhood Court for Neighborhood Suits." *Judicature*, 61, (4):185–190.

Berk, Richard A., David Rauma, Donileen R. Loseke, & Sarah F. Berk. 1982. "Throwing the Cops Back Out: The Decline of a Local Program to Make the Criminal Justice System More Responsive to Incidents of Domestic Violence." *Social Science Research*, 11:245–279.

Berk, Sarah F., & Donileen R. Loseke. 1980–81. "Handling Family Violence: Situational Determinants of Police Arrest in Domestic Disturbances." *Law and Society Review*, 15 (2):317–346.

Biddeford Journal Tribune. 1986a. "Do We Really Want to Forfeit the Right to Legal Redress?" April 26:1.

———. 1986b. "State Mediators Return for Contested Divorce Cases." April 26:1.

Bittner, Egon. 1967. "The Police on Skid Row: A Study of Peace-Keeping." *American Sociological Review*, 32:699–715.

Black, Donald. 1979. "Common Sense in the Sociology of Law." *American Sociological Review*, 44 (Feb.) :18–27.

———. 1980. *The Manners and Customs of the Police.* New York: Academic Press.

———. 1983. "Crime as Social Control." *American Sociological Review*, 48 (1):34–45.

Bordt, Rebecca L., & Michael C. Musheno. 1988. "Bureaucratic Cooptation of Informal Dispute Processing: Social Control as an Effect of Inmate Grievance Policy." *Journal of Research in Crime and Delinquency*, 25 (1):7–26.

Brillon, Yves. 1985. "Public Opinion About the Penal System: A Cynical View of Criminal Justice." In D. Gibson & J. K. Baldwin (eds.), *Law in a Cynical Society? Opinion and Law in the 1980s*, pp. 120–127. Calgary, Can.: Carswell.

Buckle, Suzanne R., & Leonard G. Buckle. 1977. *Bargaining for Justice: Case Disposition and Reform in the Criminal Courts.* New York: Praeger.

Burger, Warren. 1982. "Isn't There a Better Way?" *American Bar Association Journal*, 68:274–277.

Cain, Maureen, & Kalman Kulscar. 1981–82. "Thinking Disputes: An Essay on the Origins of the Dispute Industry." *Law and Society Review*, 16 (3):375–402.

Campbell, Bruce, & Susette M. Talarico. 1983. "Access to Legal Services: Examining Common Assumptions." *Judicature*, 66 (7):313–318.

Cavanagh, Ralph, & Austin Sarat. 1980. "Thinking About Courts: Towards and Beyond Jurisprudence of Judicial Competence." *Law and Society Review*, Winter:371–419.

Cavender, G. 1984. "Justice, Sentencing, and the Justice Model." *Criminology*, 22 (4):203–214.

Chai, C., & W. Chai. 1962. *The Changing Society of China.* New York: North American Library.

Christian, Thomas. 1985. "Mediation: The Present and Future." *Empire State Court Notes*, 3 (5).

Christie, Nils. 1977. "Conflicts as Property." *The British Journal of Criminology*, 17 (1):1–15.

———. 1986. "Images of Man in Modern Penal Law." *Contemporary Crises*, 10 (1):95–106.

Church, Thomas W. 1979. "In Defense of Bargain Justice." *Law and Society Review*, 13 (2):509–525.

Cohen, Jerome. 1982. "Symposium on the Criminal Code of the People's Republic of China." *Journal of Criminal Law and Criminology*, 73 (1, Spring):135–316.

Cohen, Jerome, S. Leng, & H. Chieu. 1977. "Symposium on Chinese Criminal Law." *Journal of Criminal Law and Criminology*, 68 (3, Sept.):323–398.

Cole, George F., & Jonathan E. Silbert. 1984. "Alternative Dispute-Resolution Mechanisms for Prisoner Grievances." *The Justice System Journal*, 9 (3):306–324.

Cooley, John W. 1986. "Arbitration vs. Mediation—Explaining the Differences." *Judicature*, 69 (5):263–269.

Coser, L. 1956. *The Functions of Social Conflict*. New York: Free Press.

Currie, Elliot. 1985. *Confronting Crime: An American Challenge*. New York: Pantheon Books.

Danzig, R. 1982. "Towards the Creation of a Complementary, Decentralized System of Criminal Justice." In R. Tomasic & M. Feeley (eds.), *Neighborhood Justice*, pp. 2–24. White Plains, N.Y.: Longman.

Danzig, Richard, & Michael J. Lowy. 1975. "Everyday Disputes and Mediation in the United States: A Reply to Professor Felstiner." *Law and Society Review*, Summer: 675–706.

Deutsch, M. 1973. *The Resolution of Conflict: Constructive and Destructive Processes*. New Haven, Conn.: Yale University Press.

Dinitz, Simon. 1983. "In Fear of Each Other." *Sociological Focus*, 16 (3, Aug.): 155–167.

Donahue, William A., Deborah Weider-Hatfield, Mark Hamilton, & Mary E. Diez. 1985. "Relational Distance in Managing Conflict." *Human Communication Research*, 11 (3):387–405.

Doob, Leonard W., & William J. Foltz. 1973. "The Belfast Workshop: An Application of Group Techniques to a Destructive Conflict." *Journal of Conflict Resolution*, 17 (3):489–512.

———. 1974. "The Impact of a Workship Upon Grass-Roots Leaders in Belfast." *Journal of Conflict Resolution*, 18 (2):237–256.

Ducker, W. M. 1983–84. "Dispute Resolution in Prisons: An Overview and Assessment." *Rutgers Law Review*, 36 (1, 2):145–178.

Durkheim, Émile. 1964. *The Rules of Sociological Method*. New York: Free Press (originally published in 1938).

Dutton, Donald G. 1987. "The Criminal Justice Response to Wife Assault." *Law and Human Behavior*, 11 (3):189–206.

———. 1988. *The Domestic Assault of Women*. Boston: Allyn & Bacon.

Edelman, Peter B. 1984. "Institutionalizing Dispute Resolution Alternatives." *The Justice System Journal*, 9 (2):134–150.

Edmonton Journal. 1988. "McSorley Evens Score With Korn." February 4:C1.

Edmonton Sun. 1986. "Hateful Man Runs Amok." August 21:1–2.

Eisenberg, Melvin Aron. 1976. "Private Ordering Through Negotiation: Dispute-Settlement and Rulemaking." *Harvard Law Review*, 89 (4):637–681.

Engel, David M. 1983. "Cases, Conflict, and Accommodation: Patterns of Legal Interaction in a Small Community." *American Bar Foundation Research*

Journal, (4):803–874.

———. 1984. "The Oven Bird's Song: Insiders, Outsiders, and Personal Injuries in an American Community." *Law and Society Review*, 18 (4):551–582.

Ewing, S. 1987. "Formal Justice and the Spirit of Capitalism: Max Weber's Sociology of Law." *Law and Society Review*, 21 (3):487–512.

Feeley, Malcolm M. 1979. "Perspectives on Plea Bargaining." *Law and Society Review*, 13 (2):199–209.

Felson, R. B., S. A. Ribner, & M. S. Siegel. 1984. "Age and the Effect of Third Parties During Criminal Violence." *Sociology and Social Research*, 68:452–462.

Felson, R. B., & H. J. Steadman. 1983. "Situational Factors in Disputes Leading to Criminal Violence." *Criminology*, 21 (1, Feb.):59–74.

Felstiner, W. 1974. "Influences of Social Organization on Dispute Processing." *Law and Society Review*, 9:63–94.

———. 1975. "Avoidance as Dispute Processing: An Elaboration." *Law and Society Review*, 9 (4):695–706.

Felstiner, W., R. L. Abel, & A. Sarat. 1980–81. "The Emergence and Transformation of Disputes: Naming, Blaming, and Claiming." *Law and Society Review*, 15 (3–4):631–654.

Felstiner, W. L. F., & L. A. Williams. 1982. "Community Mediation in Dorchester, Massachusetts." In R. Tomasic & M. M. Feeley, *Neighborhood Justice: Assessment of an Emerging Idea*, pp. 111–153. White Plains, N.Y.: Longman.

Finkelstein, Linda J. 1986. "The D.C. Multi-Door Courthouse." *Judicature*, 69 (5):305–306.

Fischer, C. 1975 May. "Towards a Subcultural Theory of Urbanism." *American Journal of Sociology*, 80:1319–1341.

Fisher, Ronald J., & James H. White. 1976. "Reducing Tensions Between Neighborhood Housing Groups: A Pilot Study in Third Party Consultation." *International Journal of Group Tensions*, 6 (3–4):41–52.

Galanter, Marc. 1983. "Reading the Landscape of Disputes: What We Know and Don't Know (and Think We Know) About Our Allegedly Contentious and Litigious Society." *UCLA Law Review*, 31 (4):4.

Geerkin, Michael R., & Walter R. Gove. 1975. "Deterrence: Some Theoretical Considerations." *Law and Society Review*, 5 (Spring):497–513.

Gibbs, Jack. 1981. *Norms, Deviance, and Social Control: Conceptual Matters*. New York: Elsevier.

———. 1985. Review Essay on Wilson and Herrnstein's "Crime and Human Nature." *Criminology*, 23 (2):381–387.

Globe and Mail. 1984a. "Mass Killer Gave Signs He'd Go Off the Deep End." September 29:A9.

———. 1984b. "Self-Defenders Tread in Unfriendly World." July 2:A9.

———. 1986. "Gunman Kills 14 Postal Workers." August 21:A1–A2.

———. 1988. "Kelleher Aims to Toughen Canada's Parole System." June 16:A1.

Goldberg, Stephen B., Eric D. Green, & Frank E. Sander. 1986. "ADR Problems and Prospects: Looking into the Future." *Judicature*, 69 (5):291–299.

Gordon, Margaret T. 1985. "The Urban Condition: 'Plates' Beneath City Surfaces and a New Research Agenda." *Urban Affairs Quarterly*, 21 (1):25–36.

Gottfredson, Michael R., & Michael J. Hindelang. 1979. "A Study of the Behavior of Law." *American Sociological Review*, 44 (Feb.):3–18.

Greider, Thomas, & Richard S. Krannich. 1985. "Neighboring Patterns. Social Support, and Rapid Growth." *Sociological Perspectives*, 28 (1):51–70.

Gulliver, P. H. 1979. *Disputes and Negotiations: A Cross-Cultural Perspective.* New York: Academic Press.

Hackler, Jim, & Antoine Garapon. 1986. "Stealing Conflicts in Juvenile Justice: Contrasting France and Canada." Discussion Paper 8, Centre for Criminological Research, University of Alberta, Edmonton.

Hagan, John. 1985. *Modern Criminology: Crime, Criminal Behavior, and Its Control.* New York: McGraw-Hill.

———. 1986. "The Unexplained Crimes of Class and Gender." In Timothy H. Hartnagel & Robert A. Silverman (eds.), *Critique and Explanation*, pp. 71–89. New Brunswick, N.J.: Transaction Press.

Hagan, John, John D. Hewitt, & Duane F. Alwin. 1979. "Ceremonial Justice: Crime and Punishment in a Loosely Coupled System." *Social Forces*, 58 (2):507–527.

Harrington, Christine B. 1985. *Shadow Justice: The Ideology and Institutionalization of Alternatives to Court.* Westport, Conn.: Greenwood Press.

Hartnagel, Timothy H. 1975. "Plea Negotiation in Canada." *Canadian Journal of Criminology*, pp. 45–56.

Henry, Stuart. 1983. *Private Justice: Towards Integrated Theorizing in the Sociology of Law.* London: Routledge & Kegan Paul.

Henshel, R. 1978. "Considerations on the Deterrence and System Capacity Models." *Criminology*, 16 (1):35–46.

Hensler, Deborah R. 1986. "What We Know and Don't Know About Court Administered Arbitration." *Judicature*, 69 (5):270–278.

Heumann, Milton, & Colin Loftin. 1979. "Mandatory Sentencing and the Abolition of Plea Bargaining: The Michigan Felony Firearm Statute." *Law and Society Review*, 13 (2):393–430.

Hilbert, R. E., & C. W. Wright. 1982. "Durkheim and Quinney on the Inevitability of Crime: A Comparative Theoretical Analysis." *Deviant Behavior*, 4:67–87.

Hirschi, Travis. 1969. *Causes of Delinquency.* Berkeley: University of California Press.

Hocker, Joyce L., & William W. Wilmot. 1985. *Interpersonal Conflict*, 2nd ed. Dubuque, Iowa: Brown.

Horrocks, Russell L. 1982. "Alternatives to the Courts in Canada." *Alberta Law Review*, 20 (2):326–334.

Jacoby, Susan. 1983. *Wild Justice.* New York: Harper & Row.

Jaffe, Peter, & C. A. Burris. 1984. "An Integrated Response to Wife Assault: A Community Model." Working Paper 1984-27. Ottawa, Can.: Solicitor General.

Johnson, Elmer. 1986. "Politics, Power and Prevention: The People's Republic of China." *Journal of Criminal Justice*, 14:449–457.

Jorgenson, David E. 1985. "Transmitting Methods of Conflict Resolution from Parents to Children: A Replication and Comparison of Blacks and Whites, Males and Females." *Social Behavior and Personality*, 13 (2): 109–117.

Katz, Jack. 1979. "Legality and Equality: Plea Bargaining in the Prosecution of

White Collar and Common Crimes." *Law and Society Review*, 13:431–459.

Kelley, Harold H., & John W. Thibaut. 1978. *Interpersonal Relations: A Theory of Interdependence*. New York: Wiley.

Kennedy, Leslie W. 1988. "Going It Alone: Unreported Crime and Individual Self-Help." *Journal of Criminal Justice*, 16 (5):403–412.

Kidd, Robert F., & Ellen F. Chayet. 1984. "Why Do Victims Fail to Report? The Psychology of Criminal Victimization." *Journal of Social Issues*, 40 (1):39–50.

Kidder, R. L. 1983. *Disputes and Negotiations: A Cross-Cultural Perspective*. New York: Academic Press.

Kinzel, C. 1985. "Edmonton Area Sampling Report 1985." Edmonton Area Series No. 41. Edmonton: Population Research Lab, University of Alberta.

Klein, Edward B., Claudewell S. Thomas, & Elizabeth C. Bellis. 1971. "When Warring Groups Meet: The Use of a Group Approach in Police-Black Community Relations." *Social Psychiatry*, 6 (2):93–99.

Klockars, Carl B. 1985. *The Idea of Police*. Beverly Hills, Calif.: Sage.

Krahn, Harvey, & Leslie W. Kennedy. 1986. "Producing Personal Safety: The Effects of Crime Rates, Police Force Size, and Fear of Crime." *Criminology*, 23 (4, Nov.): 697–710.

Krohn, Marvin D., Lonn Lanza-Kaduce, & Ronald Akers. 1984. "Community Context and Theories of Deviant Behavior: An Examination of Social Learning and Social Bonding Theories." *The Sociological Quarterly*, 25:353–371.

Lawson, Paul E. 1982. *Solving Somebody Else's Blues*. Latham, Md.: University Press of America.

Lemert, Edwin M. 1951. *Social Pathology*. New York: McGraw-Hill.

Leng, S. C. 1977. "Role of Law in the People's Republic of China as Reflecting Mao Tse-Tung's Influence." *Journal of Criminal Law*, 68 (3):356–373.

Levin, J., & J. A. Fox. 1985. *Mass Murder: America's Growing Menace*. New York: Plenum.

Macaulay, S. 1987. "Images of Law in Everyday Life: The Lessons of School, Entertainment, and Spectator Sports." *Law and Society Review*, 21 (2):185–218.

McCarthy, Belinda Rogers, & Bernard J. McCarthy. 1984. *Community-Based Corrections*. Monterey, Calif.: Cole.

McClintock, F. H. 1970. "The Dark Figure." In *Collected Studies in Criminological Research*, Strasbourg: Council of Europe, pp. 13–27, 31–34.

McEwan, Craig, & Richard J. Maiman. 1984. "Mediation in Small Claims Court: Achieving Compliance Through Consent." *Law and Society Review*, 18 (1):11–49.

McIntosh, Wayne. 1983. "Private Use of a Public Forum: A Long Range View of the Dispute Processing Role of Courts." *The American Political Science Review*, 77:991–1010.

Martin, Susan E., Lee B. Sechrest, & Robin Redner. 1981. *New Directions in the Rehabilitation of Criminal Offenders*. Washington, D.C.: National Academy Press.

Martinson, R. 1974. "What Works? Questions and Answers About Prison Reform." *Public Interest*, 35:22–54.

Mastrofski, Steven. 1983. "The Police and Noncrime Services." In Gordon Whitaker & Charles David Phillips (eds.), *Evaluating Performance of Criminal*

Justice Agencies, pp. 33–62. Beverly Hills, Calif.: Sage.

Mather, L., & B. Yngvesson. 1980–81. "Language, Audience, and the Transformation of Disputes." *Law and Society Review*, 15:775–822.

Maynard, Douglas W. 1984. *Inside Plea Bargaining: The Language of Negotiation.* New York: Plenum.

———. 1985. "On the Functions of Social Conflict Among Children." *American Sociological Review*, 50 (Apr.):207–223.

Mednick, S. A., W. F. Gabrielli, Jr., & B. Hutchings. 1984 "Genetic Influence in Criminal Convictions: Evidence from on Adoption Cohort." *Science* 224:891–894.

Meier, R., & W. Johnson. 1977. "Deterrence as Social Control: The Legal and Extralegal Production of Conformity." *American Sociological Review*, 42 (Apr.):292–304.

Merry, Sally E. 1979. "Going to Court: Strategies of Dispute Management in an American Urban Neighborhood." *Law and Society Review*, 13 (Summer):891–925.

———. 1981. *Urban Danger: Life in a Neighborhood of Strangers.* Philadephia: Temple University Press.

———. 1982a. "Defining 'Success' in the Neighborhood Justice Movement." In Roman Tomasic & Malcolm M. Feeley (eds.), *Neighborhood Justice: Assessment of an Emerging Idea*, pp. 172–192. New York: Longman.

———. 1982b. "The Social Organization of Mediation in Nonindustrial Societies: Implications for Informal Community Justice in America." In Richard Abel (ed.), *The Politics of Informal Justice*, pp. 17–45. New York: Academic Press.

Merry, S. E., & S. S. Silbey. 1984. "What Do Plaintiffs Want? Reexamining the Concept of Disputes." *Justice System Journal*, 9 (2):151–178.

Miller, R. E., & A. Sarat. 1980–81. "Grievances, Claims, and Disputes: Assessing the Adversary Culture." *Law and Society Review*, 15 (3–4):525–565.

Mischel, W. 1968. *Personality and Assessment.* New York: Wiley.

Mnookin, Robert H., & Lewis Kornhauser. 1979. "Bargaining in the Shadow of the Law: The Case of Divorce." *Yale Law Journal*, 88:950–997.

Monkkonen, Eric H. 1983. "The Organized Response to Crime in Nineteenth- and Twentieth-Century America." *Journal of Interdisciplinary History*, 14 (1):113–128.

Moore, C., & J. Brown. 1981. *Community Versus Crime.* London: Bedford Square Press.

Moore, Robert J. 1985. "Reflections of Canadians on the Law and the Legal System: Legal Research Institute Survey of Respondents in Montreal, Toronto, and Winnipeg." In Dale Gibson & Janet K. Baldwin (eds.), *Law in a Cynical Society? Opinion and Law in the 1980s*, pp. 41–88. Calgary, Can.: Carswell.

Moore, Sally Falk. 1973. "Law and Social Change: The Semi-autonomous Social Field as an Appropriate Subject of Study." *Law and Society Review*, Summer: 719–746.

Morris, Norval, & Gordon Hawkins. 1969. *The Honest Politician's Guide to Crime Control.* Chicago: University of Chicago Press.

Nader, Laura. 1984. "From Disputing to Complaining." In Donald Black (ed.), *Toward a General Theory of Social Control*, Vol. 1, pp. 71–94. Orlando, Fla.:

Academic Press.

Nader, L., & L. Singer. 1976. "Dispute Resolution and the Law in the Future: What are the Choices?" *California State Law Journal*, 51:281–286.

Nader, Laura, & H. F. Todd (eds.). 1978. *The Disputing Process—Law in Ten Societies*. New York: Columbia University Press.

Nettler, G. 1984a. *Explaining Crime*, 3rd ed. New York: McGraw-Hill.

———. 1984b. "On 'Rehabilitation.'" *Law and Human Behavior*, 8, (3/4):383–393.

New York Times. 1986a. "An Alternative to Litigation." Mar. 4:D2.

———. 1986b. "Workers Return to Slaying Scene." Aug. 22:1–2.

Nielsen, Marianne. 1982. "Native People and the Criminal Justice System: The Role of the Native Courtworker." *Canadian Legal Aid Bulletin*, 5 (2):55–63.

Palenski, Joseph E. 1984. "The Use of Mediation By Police." *Mediation Quarterly*, 5:31–38.

Palmer, John W. 1975a. "The Night Prosecutor." *Judicature*, 59 (1):23–27.

———. 1975b. "Pre-Arrest Diversion: The Night Prosecutor's Program in Columbus, Ohio." *Crime and Delinquency*, 21 (2):100–108.

Paternoster, Raymond, Linda E. Saltzman, Gordon P. Waldo, & Theodore G. Chiricos. 1983. "Perceived Risk and Social Control: Do Sanctions Really Deter?" *Law and Society Review*, 17 (3):457–479.

Pence, E. 1985. *Criminal Justice Response to Domestic Assault Cases: A Guide to Policy Development*. Duluth, Minn.: Domestic Abuse Intervention Project.

People. 1985. "Shoot Out in the Street," 23 (11, Sept. 5):88–96.

Pipkin, Ronald M., & Janet Rifkin. 1984. "The Social Organization in Alternative Dispute Resolution: Implications for Professionalization of Mediation." *The Justice System Journal*, 9 (2):204–227.

Pontell, H. N. 1978. "Deterrence: Theory and Practice." *Criminology*, 16 (1):3–22.

Pritchard, David. 1986. "Homicide and Bargained Justice: The Agenda Setting Effect of Crime News on Prosecutors." *Public Opinion Quarterly*, 50:143–159.

Pruet, George W., & Henry R. Glick. 1986. "Social Environment, Public Opinion, and Judicial Policymaking: A Search for Judicial Representation." *American Politics Quarterly*, 14 (1–2):5–33.

Quinney, Richard. 1974. *Critique of Legal Order*. Boston: Little, Brown.

Reider, Jonathan. 1984. "The Social Organization of Vengeance." In Donald Black (ed.), *Toward a General Theory of Social Control*, Vol. 1, pp. 131–162.

Reiss, Albert J., Jr. 1984. "Consequences of Compliance and Deterrence Models of Law Enforcement for the Exercise of Police Discretion." *Law and Contemporary Problems*, 47 (4):83–122.

Rich, Elwood M. 1980. "An Experiment with Judicial Mediation." *American Bar Association Journal*, 66 (May):530.

Roehl, Janice A., & Royer F. Cook. 1985. "Issues in Mediation: Rhetoric and Reality Revisited." *Journal of Social Issues*, 41 (2):161–178.

Rumbart, Ruben G., & Egon Bittner. 1979. "Changing Conceptions of the Police Role: A Sociological Review." In N. Morris & M. Tonry (eds.), *Crime and Justice: An Annual Review of Research*, Vol. 1, pp. 239–288. Chicago: University of Chicago Press.

Ryan, John Paul, & James J. Alfini. 1979. "Trial Judges' Participation in Plea Bargaining: An Empirical Perspective." *Law and Society Review*, 9:479–507.

Salas, Luis, & Ronald Schneider. 1979. "Evaluating the Dade County Citizen Dispute Settlement Program." *Judicature*, 63 (4):174–183.

Sander, Frank. 1982. "Varieties of Dispute Processing." In Roman Tomasic & Malcolm Feeley (eds.), *Neighborhood Justice: An Assessment of an Emerging Idea*, pp. 25–43. White Plains, N.Y.: Longman.

———. 1984. "Alternative Dispute Resolution in the Law School Curriculum: Opportunities and Obstacles." *Journal of Legal Education*, 34 (2):229–236.

Sarat, A. 1976. "Alternative in Dispute Processing: Litigation in a Small Claims Court." *Law and Society Review*, 9 (Spring):339–375.

Sarat, Austin, & Joel B. Grossman. 1975. "Courts and Conflict Resolution: Problems in the Mobilization of Adjudication." *American Political Science Review*, 69:1200–1217.

Scarman, Lord. 1981. "Report of the Brixton Disorders; 10–12 April, 1981." Cmnd. 8247, London: HMSO.

Scheingold, Stuart A. 1984. *The Politics of Law and Order: Street Crime and Public Policy*. White Plains, N.Y.: Longman.

Schulhofer, Stephen J. 1984. "Inside Plea Bargaining." *Harvard Law Review*, 97 (Mar.):1037–1107.

———. 1988. "Criminal Justice Discretion as a Regulatory System." *Journal of Legal Studies*, 17 (Jan.):43–82.

Schur, Edwin M. 1965. *Crimes Without Victims*. Englewood Cliffs, N.J.: Prentice-Hall.

Scull, Andrew. 1984. *Decarceration: Community Treatment and the Deviant—A Radical View*. Cambridge: Polity Press.

Sellin, Thorsten. 1938. *Culture Conflict and Crime*. New York: Science Research Council.

Selva, Lance H., & Robert M. Bohm. 1987. "A Critical Examination of the Information Experiment in the Administration of Justice." *Crime and Social Justice*, 29:43–57.

Shaffer, Evelyn B. 1980. *Community Policing*. London: Croom Helm.

Sherman, Lawrence W. 1984. "Experiments in Police Discretion: Scientific Boon or Dangerous Knowledge." *Law and Contemporary Problems*, 47 (4):61–81.

Sherman, Lawrence W., & Richard A. Berk. 1984. "The Specific Deterrent Effects of Arrest for Domestic Assault." *American Sociological Review*, 49 (Apr.): 261–272.

Silberman, M. 1976. "Toward a Theory of Criminal Deterrence." *American Sociological Review*, 41 (June):442–461.

Silbey, Susan, & Austin Sarat. 1987. "Critical Traditions in Law and Society Research." *Law and Society Review*, 21 (1):165–174.

Silverman, Robert A., & Leslie W. Kennedy. 1988. "Women Who Kill Their Children." *Violence and Victims*, 3 (2):113–127.

Skogan, Wesley G. 1984. "Reporting Crimes to the Police: The Status of World Research." *Journal of Crime and Delinquency,* 21 (2):113–137.

———. 1987. *Disorder and Community Decline*. Evanston, Ill.: Center for Urban and Policy Research.

Skolnick, Jerome. 1966. *Justice Without Trial*. New York: Wiley.

Smith, Douglas A. 1984. "The Organization Context of Legal Control." *Criminology*, 22 (1):19–38.

———. 1986. "The Plea Bargaining Controversy." *Journal of Criminal Law and Criminology*, 77 (3):949–968.

———. 1987. "Police Response to Interpersonal Violence: Defining the Parameters of Legal Control." *Social Forces*, 65 (3):767–782.

Smith, Douglas A., & Jody R. Klein. 1984. "Police Control of Interpersonal Disputes." *Social Problems*, 31 (4):468–481.

Smith, Susan J. 1983. "Crime and the Structure of Social Relations." *Transactions of the Institute of British Geographers N.S.*, 9:427–442.

Snyder, Frederick E. 1978. "Crime and Community Mediation—The Boston Experience: A Preliminary Report on the Dorchester Urban Court Program." *Wisconsin Law Review*, pp. 737–795.

Stagner, R. 1971. "Personality Dynamics and Social Conflict." In C. G. Smith (ed.), *Conflict Resolution: Contributions of the Behavioral Sciences*, pp. 98–109. South Bend, Ind.: University of Notre Dame Press.

Statsky, William P. 1974. "Community Courts: Decentralizing Juvenile Jurisprudence." *Capital University Law Review*, 3 (1):1–31.

Sternberg, Robert J., & Lawrence J. Soriano. 1984. "Styles of Conflict Resolution." *Journal of Personality and Social Psychology*, 47 (1):115–126.

Straus, Murray. 1985. The Index of Legitimate Violence. Unpublished manuscript, University of New Hampshire, Durham.

Strauss, Anselm. 1978. *Negotiation: Varieties, Contexts, and Social Order*. San Francisco: Jossey-Bass.

Stulberg, Joseph B. 1975. "A Civil Alternative to Criminal Prosecution." *Albany Law Review*, 39 (3):359–376.

Sutherland, Edwin H. 1929. "Crime and the Conflict Process." *Journal of Juvenile Research*, 13:38–48.

Suttles, Gerald. 1972. *The Social Construction of Communities*. Chicago: University of Chicago Press.

Taylor, Ian, Paul Walton, & Jock Young. 1973. *The New Criminology: For a Social Theory of Deviance*. London: Routledge & Kegan Paul.

Teevan, James. 1976. "Deterrent Effects of Punishment: Subjective Measures Continued." *Canadian Journal of Criminology and Corrections*, 18:156–159.

Terhune, K. 1970. "The Effects of Personality in Cooperation and Conflict." In P. Swingle (ed.), *The Structure of Conflict*, pp. 193–234. New York: Academic Press.

Tittle, Charles. 1980. *Sanctions and Social Deviance: The Question of Deterrence*. New York: Praeger.

Tomasic, Roman. 1982. "Mediation as an Alternative to Adjudication: Rhetoric and Reality in the Neighborhood Justice Movement." In Roman Tomasic & Malcolm M. Feeley (eds.), *Neighborhood Justice: Assessment of an Emerging Idea*, pp. 215–248. White Plains, N.Y.: Longman.

Turk, Austin. 1966. "Conflict and Criminality." *American Sociological Review*, 31:338–352.

———. 1976. "Law as a Weapon in Social Conflict." *Social Problems*, 23 (3,

Feb.):276–291.

Unger, Donald G., & Abraham Wandersman. 1985. "The Importance of Neighbors: The Social, Cognitive, and Affective Components of Neighboring." *American Journal of Community Psychology*, 13 (2):139–169.

Vidmar, Neil. 1985. "An Assessment of Mediation in Small Claims Court." *Journal of Social Issues*, 41 (2):127–144.

Visher, Christy A. 1983. "Gender, Police Arrest Decisions, and Notions of Chivalry." *Criminology*, 21 (1):5–28.

Vold, George B., & Thomas J. Bernard. 1986. *Theoretical Criminology*. New York: Oxford University Press.

Williams, Kirk, & Richard Hawkins. 1986. "Perceptual Research on General Deterrence: A Critical Review." *Law and Society Review*, 20 (4):545–572.

Wilson. James Q. 1968. *Varieties of Police Behavior*. Cambridge, Mass.: Harvard University Press.

———. 1983. *Thinking About Crime*. New York: Vintage Books.

Wilson, James Q., & Richard J. Herrnstein. 1985. *Crime and Human Nature*. New York: Simon & Schuster.

Wirth, Louis. 1938. "Urbanism as a Way of Life." *American Journal of Sociology*, 44:1–24.

Wolfgang, M., & Franco Ferracuti. 1967. *The Subculture of Violence*. London: Tavistock.

Woods, Laurie. 1985. Mediation: A Backlash to Women's Progress on Family Law Issues in the Courts and Legislatures. Unpublished paper, National Center on Women and Family Law, New York.

Zimring, Frank E., & G. J. Hawkins. 1973. *Deterrence: The Legal Threat in Crime Control*. Chicago: University of Chicago Press.

Author Index

Abel, Richard, 33, 65, 79, 81–83
Adler, Peter, 65
Akers, Ronald, 23
Alderson, John, 100
Alfini, James, 116
Alschuler, Albert, 116, 118, 119
Alwin, Duane, 120
Aubert, Vilhelm, 44, 115, 126
Auberbach, Jerold, 112, 113

Baldwin, John, 118
Bard, Morton, 93
Beer, Jennifer, 67
Bellis, Elizabeth, 99
Beresford, Robert, 72
Berk, Richard, 16, 53, 79, 94, 95
Berk, Sarah, 94
Bernard, Thomas, 7, 12, 15
Bittner, Egon, 93, 97
Black, Donald, 20, 21, 35, 37, 41, 42,
    51, 52, 55, 91, 92, 97, 99
Bohm, Robert, 81, 82
Bordt, Rebecca, 75
Brillon, Yves, 52
Brown, John, 101
Buckle, Leonard, 118

Buckle, Suzanne, 118
Burger, Warren, 105, 114, 127

Cain, Maureen, 1, 9, 43–45
Campbell, Bruce, 112
Cavanagh, Ralph, 83, 106, 107, 121
Cavender, G., 58
Chai, C., 9
Chai, W., 9
Chayet, Ellen, 6
Chieu, H., 10, 11
Christian, Thomas, 73
Christie, Nils, 33, 35, 43, 44, 71, 82,
    111, 126
Church, Thomas, 116, 117
Cohen, Jerome, 10, 11
Cole, George, 75
Cook, Royer, 71, 73, 78, 79, 81, 82
Cooley, John, 66, 67
Cooper, Jill, 72
Coser, Lewis, 12, 20, 21, 107
Currie, Elliot, 4, 15, 52, 54, 55, 59, 60

Danzig, Richard, 44, 65, 68, 69, 72, 76
Deutsch, M., 19
Dinitz, Simon, 75

143

Subject Index